Praise for *Hip Kosher*

"Ronnie Fein's newest cookbook, *Hip Kosher: 175 Ea[...]*
Prepare Recipes for Today's Kosher Cooks offers creativ[...]
for the modern kosher family. Fein makes her mark by
highlighting the interesting ingredients, and her helpful hints
are generously offered in nearly every recipe. *Hip Kosher* will be
a terrific addition to the kitchen of any home-cook!"

> —Jeff Nathan, executive chef of Abigael's on Broadway and Jeff
> Nathan Events, chef/host of television's "New Jewish Cuisine,"
> and author of *Adventures in Jewish Cooking* and *Jeff Nathan's*
> *Family Suppers*

"Ronnie Fein is a well-seasoned cooking teacher and cookbook
author, and I am anxious to try all of the recipes in *Hip Kosher*.
The notes and tips she offers on each recipe make the book a
great find!"

> —Sally Maraventano, cookbook author, chef/owner of Cucina
> Casalinga, Regional Italian Cooking School

"If you think kosher cooking means hours and hours in the
kitchen and heavy, wintry food, think again! Ronnie Fein has a
wealth of talent and experience, and she is just plain fun, and
so is her food. It's fast, fresh, bright, and summery. This is
kosher cooking for everyone who loves good food."

> —Melanie Barnard, award-winning cookbook author of
> *Marinades: The Secret of Grilling*

"*Hip Kosher* offers simple, quick recipes featuring fresh
ingredients, making it a welcome addition to anyone's
cookbook library, whether they cook kosher or not. Helpful
guides with regard to kosher cooking are sprinkled throughout
the book, and each chapter is chock-full of suggested
shortcuts, menu ideas, and other tips."

> —*Austin Chronicle*

"*Hip Kosher* features flavors from around the world in simple recipes that are more indicative of today's diverse kosher consumers and ingredients."

—The Jewish Week

"Fein, a Connecticut-based author, food writer and cooking school director, has a love for flavors and spices from around the world and an eye for what people want to eat today."

—Chicago Tribune

"The proof that her recipes are easy is in the titles…and it's in the recipe directions: most of them are single paragraphs. [Fein] uses all sections of the international foods aisle for this book, yet all the recipes are kosher."

—Washington Post

"Lots of simple, quick, appealing modern fare can be found in this book relying on supermarket accessible ingredients."

—Los Angeles Daily News

"Modern kosher-American food in Fein's book takes some of the best elements of several cuisines and combines them."

—Worcester Telegram & Gazette

"If you are new to kosher food or if you are a kosher food veteran who would enjoy a fresh collection of current, delicious and healthy kosher recipes that are easy-to-prepare, then *Hip Kosher* may make a wonderful addition to your kitchen library."

—Giora Shimoni, *About.com*

ABOUT THE AUTHOR

Ronnie Fein has been a freelance food and lifestyle writer since 1980. She currently writes regular features for the food and community sections of daily newspapers, including the *Advocate* and *Greenwich Time*, which are part of MediaNews-Hearst newspapers; many of these articles appear in other publications throughout the United States and in international editions, as well as online. Ronnie Fein has written articles for *Newsday*, *Cook's Illustrated*, *Consumer's Digest*, *Connecticut* magazine, and many other publications; is the author of two previous cookbooks; and was a contributing editor to *The New Cook's Catalogue*. She also operates the Ronnie Fein School of Creative Cooking in Stamford, Connecticut, where she lives with her husband. She has two married daughters and three grandchildren.

ALSO BY RONNIE FEIN

The Complete Idiot's Guide to Cooking Basics
The Complete Idiot's Guide to American Cooking

HIP KOSHER

175 EASY-TO-PREPARE RECIPES FOR TODAY'S KOSHER COOKS

RONNIE FEIN

Da Capo

LIFE
LONG

A Member of the Perseus Books Group

For my children
Meredith and Gregory,
Gillian, and Jesse,
the hippest cooks I know

Copyright © 2008 by Ronnie Fein

Designed by Jeff Williams

Library of Congress Cataloging-in-Publication Data
Fein, Ronnie.
    Hip kosher : 175 easy-to-prepare recipes for today's kosher cooks / Ronnie Fein.
        p. cm.
    ISBN-13: 978-1-60094-053-8 (pbk. : alk. paper)
    ISBN-10: 1-60094-053-6 (pbk. : alk. paper) 1. Jewish cookery. 2. Cookery, American. 3. Cookery, International. I. Title.

TX724.F3718 2008
641.5973—dc22

                                                                        2007045786

Published by Da Capo Press
A member of the Perseus Books Group
www.dacapopress.com

Da Capo Press books are available at special discounts for bulk purchases in the United States by corporations, institutions, and other organizations. For more information, please contact the Special Markets Department at the Perseus Books Group, 2300 Chestnut Street, Suite 200, Philadelphia, PA 19103, or call (800) 255–1514, or e-mail special.markets@perseusbooks.com.

2 3 4 5 6 7 8 9

CONTENTS

SANDWICHES 165

VEGETABLES 179

DESSERTS 201

MISCELLANEOUS BASICS 223

INTRODUCTION

In the 1960s a man named Whitey Ruben, who owned a small bakery in Brooklyn, wanted a bigger market for his baked goods and sought a good idea to broaden sales. His search led him to the Doyle Dane Bernbach advertising agency, where Bill Bernbach made a suggestion that surprised him. Bernbach suggested that the bakery's Jewish rye bread be more widely marketed to non-Jews.

The rest, as they say, is history. The legendary ad, "You don't have to be Jewish to love Levy's real Jewish rye" was a sensation and made a fortune for all concerned, as the bread became a bestseller.

To paraphrase that famous slogan, you don't have to be Jewish to eat or cook kosher food. In fact, while the last ten years have seen a dramatic upsurge in kosher cuisine and double-digit increases in annual sales of kosher products, the people who are fueling this trend are not necessarily Jewish. Muslims, Seventh Day Adventists, and Jehovah's Witnesses account for some of the growth. More interestingly, though, the trend is also being driven by people for whom eating kosher is not a faith-based mandate. The newest kosher crowd is made up of a wide variety of people including vegetarians, vegans, those with certain allergies or lactose intolerance, people who describe themselves as health conscious, people who are concerned with animal welfare, those interested in organic foods, and lastly, many who believe that being kosher will help them connect more spiritually to the food they are eating. As a group, these diners all believe that following *kashruth*, the Jewish dietary laws, is a cleaner, purer, more humane, or healthier way to eat.

Kosher restaurants, responding to the shifting tastes of this surging demand, now serve eclectic foods such as sushi, Thai spring rolls, miso-glazed sea bass, and chicken fajitas. Food manufacturers have added thousands of kosher products to their lines and have redesigned their advertising messages to address the current tastes of this more diverse audience. Supermarkets have expanded their kosher food sections. Kosher-certified Asian, Caribbean, Latin, and other ethnic ingredients are readily available, giving kosher cooks access to wasabi powder, hoisin sauce, harissa, salsa, and ancho chile pepper, among other items.

In the past, kosher cooks in America were primarily of Eastern European Jewish descent, but today's kosher cooks come from divergent backgrounds. Many kosher cooks who are Jewish are generations away from Old World culinary traditions when it comes to their everyday cooking. Like all Americans, kosher home cooks have been exposed to the international tastes that influence modern American cooking trends.

Although traditional ethnic foods are usually welcome and expected for Jewish holiday dinners, when it comes to everyday meals, today's more modern and sophisticated kosher home cooks prefer to cook more modern and sophisticated American food. They watch food shows on television and browse through chef cookbooks for the inspiration provided by elaborate, professional-style dishes. But at the heart of it, kosher home cooks are *home cooks*. They mainly want advice and recipes for day-to-day cooking. They are like most other hurried and harried Americans: they want to prepare flavorful meals that are easy, time saving, and forgiving.

That's why I have written this book. I am frequently asked by my students and many who have attended discussion groups that I lead how to adapt modern recipes for the kosher kitchen. I wanted to make it easier for them, for anyone—whether for religious or spiritual reasons, or for any reason whatsoever—who wishes to follow the kosher dietary laws to prepare recipes that reflect where the American culinary culture is today.

Adapting local cuisine to kashruth is nothing new. For millennia, kosher cooks have followed the cooking styles of the places where they lived, changing recipes to meet kosher requirements. This is no less true in America, where the foods that we eat reveal a rich and varied cultural heritage. Some years ago my grandson Zev and the other children in his preschool class were asked to bring in a dish that reflected their ethnic backgrounds. Zev picked challah, a traditional Jewish favorite, but only after finding out that the two other Jewish children in the class had already decided to bring his first choices: chicken nuggets or apple pie. Their families, like ours, do not rely on our traditional ethnic fare on a daily basis. We eat things like chicken nuggets and apple pie, like many other Americans. We prepare the same foods as our neighbors, the same foods that other Americans eat every day throughout the United States.

Modern American cuisine includes foods that embrace Latin, Asian, African, and European influences. It's a little Italian, a little Chinese, a little Mexican, a little Moroccan, and so on. Modern kosher-American food should do the same. The recipes in this book underscore our rich culinary heritage and so I've included recipes that illustrate the variety of our ethnicity: Chicken with Dates and Toasted Almonds (page 130) from the Middle East; Beef Kebabs with Quick Pebre Sauce (page 103), a Chilean specialty; Italian-style Bread and Tomato Soup (page 26), and Mexican Huevos Rancheros (page 152), among others. I've also included some old-fashioned "American" classics like Baked Alaska (page 212), updated to consider current-day tastes and time constraints. Then, too, there are many recipes that reflect the way modern American cooks take the best elements of several cuisines and combine them into one delicious recipe or take advantage of the bountiful supply of fresh meats and produce and packaged goods we can buy here: Grilled Salmon with Pineapple-Mango Salsa (page 83), Lamburgers with Sun-Dried Tomato Mayo (page 174), Stir-Fried

Couscous with Chicken, Dried Apricots, and Pistachio Nuts (page 75), Pumpkin Bisque with Curry and Pear (page 29), Roasted Asparagus with Wasabi Mayonnaise (page 190), Edamame Succotash and Feta Cheese Quiche (page 155), and Mexican Hot Chocolate Brownies (page 210), to name a few. It's hip kosher, with stylish, up-to-date recipes that will help you expand your culinary repertoire and keep dinner interesting.

I've included more than 175 recipes in this book (look for the recipes within recipes). Each relies on kosher ingredients that are widely available—I bought all of the ingredients I needed locally. I did much of my shopping, including buying fresh meats and poultry, in the kinds of old-fashioned supermarkets that you'll find throughout the country, although on occasion I traveled to a kosher butcher when I couldn't find what I wanted in the local store. I always buy seafood at a fishmonger, where the fish seems fresher and more visually appealing, and while I sometimes buy produce at a supermarket or specialty store like Whole Foods or a local organic place, I shop at a farmers' market whenever I can because that's where I find the biggest variety of fruits and vegetables (including some unusual items that never show up in the stores) that I know are fresh. Each of the recipes that I've chosen is designed to satisfy busy people who don't want to spend hours in the kitchen. I did not include meat stews or many braised dishes for the very reason that these require long, slow simmering. Most of the recipes call for broiling, grilling, pan sautéing, stir-frying, or other quick-cooking methods. There are a few recipes for braised fish, chicken, and vegetables that, unlike meat, do not require long cooking times. Recipes for roasted foods use ingredients (like a half turkey breast) that cook within a relatively short time.

I've divided the recipes into categories that correspond to courses of the meal (soups, meats, and so on) and also reflect the kosher requirement of separating meat and milk products. Where a small change here or there in a recipe will change a category from meat to dairy (or vice versa), I have indicated the changes to be made. All the recipes are accommodating that is, they leave room for human error. I've also written lots of extra tips in sidebars that note variations on recipes, updates on the classics, and helpful preparation hints about ingredients and tools. Many of the recipes will give you menu suggestions. Most of the recipes can be prepared and cooked within a short time; a few suggest marinating or some other time-consuming step.

I should mention that although there are rules that clearly distinguish between what is kosher and what is not, it is also the case that people regard their commitment to kashruth in a variety of ways. This book is not intended to point fingers or to create guilt. It is merely a means by which kosher home cooks can find easy, modern, interesting recipes to make at home. There's a world of food out there to help every kosher cook prepare delicious meals at home. Take advantage of it! Of course, if you ever have a question about whether a product or particular food is kosher it is always advisable to consult your local rabbinic authority. Or e-mail the Webbe Rebbe at kosherq@ou.org, a very helpful resource.

WHAT DOES KOSHER MEAN?

We use the word *kosher* in common parlance when we want to say that something is acceptable, legitimate, aboveboard, okay. But kosher derives from *kashruth*, a Hebrew word that concerns dietary laws found in the Old Testament. It has to do with eating.

Or does it?

A commitment to kosher begins with the Jewish dietary laws but goes beyond strict obedience to biblical enactments and rabbinical edicts. Although the dietary laws focus on food, they also relate to the ethical treatment of animals and respect for life. Being kosher means making spiritual and lifestyle choices. People who are kosher conduct themselves in accordance with the dietary laws. The food they eat nourishes them physically, and spiritually as well. It is fit and proper, legitimate, acceptable, okay.

When food is kosher it doesn't mean it has been blessed by a rabbi. Blessings are not the relevant criteria. Kosher foods are those set forth in the Old Testament books of Leviticus and Deuteronomy as well as in the various decrees handed down by rabbinical authorities over the centuries. The rules are complicated and not always as straightforward as they seem. Those who were raised in a kosher household presumably are familiar with what is kosher and what is not. But for those who weren't, for the uninitiated and the newly initiated trying to find their way through the complexities of what it means to be kosher, the following sections will be a useful guide. I have also pointed out those areas in which conflicting opinions exist regarding kosher products. If you are in doubt about whether a food or ingredient is kosher it is important always to consult your local authority on *halakha,* which literally means "the path one walks" but is interpreted as "Jewish law." Your best bet is to consult a rabbi through a local synagogue.

WHAT IS KOSHER FOOD?

Kosher foods are separated into meat, dairy, and a third category, *pareve*, which are neutral foods that include vegetables, fruits, grains, eggs, and fish. But not all meat, dairy, and pareve products are kosher. Beyond the categories and lists of what is permissible or prohibited, to be kosher the food must also be treated properly. Meats and poultry that are eligible to be kosher must be slaughtered in a specific manner. Prepared or processed items must be inspected and certified by a rabbinic expert, called a *mashgiach*. The expert checks every detail involved in production. Every ingredient must be kosher and all the manufacturing equipment must be used only for kosher foods. A mashgiach typically makes unannounced on-site visits to be sure the premises and all aspects of production are acceptable. If the particular item and its manufacture have met the expert's standards, a *hekhsher*, an identifiable symbol, is placed on the label. Although the Orthodox Union (OU) logo is likely to be the most familiar hekhsher (the letter U inside a circle), there are dozens of certification symbols, such as Star-K (the letter K inside a 5-pointed star) and the Organized Kashrus Laboratories (the letter K inside a circle). Some people will only eat products certified by the OU, others accept any legitimate hekhsher. You might see a single letter K appearing on a label, but that is not a hekhsher and has no value. A letter can't be a copyrighted logo so a single letter K without any other distinguishing mark doesn't tell you if the food was inspected and approved (or by whom).

You can find a list of hekhshers online at www.kosherquest.org.

Meat

To be kosher, meat must come from an animal that has cloven (split) hooves and chews its cud. Animals that have these two features are not carnivorous. Commentaries on the reasons for this rule suggest that by refraining from eating animals that prey on other animals, people who follow kashruth will be more reluctant to take a life unnecessarily.

Kosher animals include cows (beef and veal), buffalo, sheep (lamb and mutton), goats, and deer (venison). Pork isn't kosher because pigs don't chew their cud. Rabbits and hares aren't kosher because they don't have split hooves.

For an animal to be kosher, its slaughtering must be performed by a *shochet*, a trained professional, in a way that will inflict minimal pain and the least amount of suffering to the animal. The shochet uses a special razor-sharp knife that has no nicks or flaws and severs the animal's trachea, esophagus, and jugular vein with one stroke, causing near-instantaneous death.

After slaughter the internal organs must be inspected for any abnormalities that would render the animal *treif* (nonkosher). Specifically, the lungs are examined for adhesions. Not all lung adhesions are forbidden, yet you might see the term *glatt* kosher in reference to meat. *Glatt* is a Yiddish word that means "smooth" and indicates that the animal's lungs were completely smooth, without any adhesions at all, even "allowable" ones. Today the term *glatt* or *glatt kosher* has taken on a broader meaning and is a hyperbolic way of saying "very kosher." But that is a misconception; the word has a specific application to meat.

The kosher dietary laws forbid eating certain fats of cattle, sheep, and goat. Because removing the fats from the hind legs and loins of these animals is complicated and expensive, the hindquarters are usually sold as nonkosher meat. Sirloin, strip, and flank steaks, filets mignons, round steaks, and roasts as well as leg of lamb are not kosher. Kosher cuts are most often limited to those from the forequarter: rib, chuck, shoulder, brisket, and shank among them.

Some kosher butchers sell meats with names similar to nonkosher cuts, such as London broil or filet. But if it's kosher, it will be cut from permitted portions, carved to resemble the nonkosher cuts. Good examples are the filet split, which looks like filet mignon but is cut from the chuck, and strip steak, which looks like loin but is also chuck. Tournedos are medallions of beef cut from the eye of the rib, not from the tenderloin, as it is with nonkosher meat.

The rules of kashruth also forbid consuming blood. For that reason, after an animal has been slaughtered, its carcass is left to hang to allow the blood to drain. The meat is salted within seventy-two hours to extract remaining blood, and rinsed several times. Broiling is an alternative method for removing blood—and the only way to rid liver of blood—but kosher soaked and salted meat is usually widely available. It isn't necessary to cook kosher meat well done. Any juices that remain after the koshering process are okay to eat.

Even though it is rinsed, kosher meat retains salt, so as a culinary matter it is best to taste a small amount first and add salt only as necessary when preparing recipes. The recipes in this book assume you'll be doing that.

Meat and Dairy

A famous passage in the scriptures says, "Do not boil a kid in its mother's milk." This phrase has been interpreted as a moral lesson against being cruel to animals or taking innocent life and is the basis for the kashruth rule that prohibits cooking or eating meat and dairy together. Veal Parmesan and Chili con Carne with shredded cheddar could never be kosher.

And there is no such thing as a kosher cheeseburger (except that these days there are nondairy soy "cheeses"—soy is pareve—that taste very much like the real thing).

Kosher kitchens are equipped with separate dishes, utensils, and cookware, one for meat, the other for dairy. Some authorities permit dishes made of glass, which isn't porous, to be used for either meat or dairy; others prohibit this practice.

The prohibition against eating meat and dairy together has a few further wrinkles. It is necessary to wait some time after eating meat to eat dairy. For example, the standard rule is that six hours must elapse before you can have an ice cream sundae after a steak dinner. (There are exceptions in different communities and for certain health reasons.) The reverse is not the case, however. You may eat meat after having dairy foods (but it is necessary to rinse your hands and mouth) except in the case of cheese that has been aged for six months or longer. In that case, the six-hour waiting period applies.

Poultry

The rules about whether poultry is kosher are not as clear-cut as they are with meat. Twenty-four forbidden birds are mentioned in the Old Testament, but no specific identifying features are given. Because there have been so many translations from the original Hebrew text no one is sure whether the listed species are the same ones known by those names today. Through the centuries, deciding which birds are kosher has generally been a matter of tradition. A bird is kosher if it has always been considered so in one community or another and is not among the twenty-four forbidden species. Chicken, Cornish hens, domestic geese, and duck can be made kosher; there is some disagreement about quail, doves, pigeons (squab), and pheasant, but that may be because those species are not kosher-slaughtered commercially. Interestingly, turkey's kosher status was once in question, but it is now universally permitted. In fact, in recent years some authorities have given their blessing to certain breeds of wild turkey.

On the other hand, birds of prey are among the species that are forbidden. They are not and never will be kosher. The prohibition against eating vicious animals is a reminder not to be vicious ourselves.

As with meat, for poultry to be considered kosher, it must be slaughtered by a shochet in a specific ritualistic manner that causes the least amount of pain to the animal. After slaughter, it is soaked and salted within twenty-four hours to draw out the blood. You'll find that because it has been brined, kosher poultry is full of flavor and is remarkably succulent, but, as with meat, you'll need to be judicious about the amount of salt you add to recipes.

Because birds are considered meat, you can't prepare or serve them with dairy. A kosher recipe for chicken or turkey would never include cheese or use a yogurt marinade.

Fish

There is no reference in the Bible to any particular fish being kosher or not but the Bible does describe the characteristics of the kind that may be eaten. The rules actually cover all marine life but they are commonly referred to as "fish."

Basically, to be kosher, fish must have fins and scales. The scales must also be of a type that can be removed without destroying the animal's skin. Shellfish including shrimp, lobster, scallops, crab, oysters, mussels, and clams, and other mollusks such as octopus and squid are not kosher because they have no fins or scales. Catfish and monkfish don't have scales; shark, eel, and some turbots have scales, but not the kind that can be removed easily, so these are nonkosher. There is some difference of opinion when it comes to swordfish and sturgeon, having to do with the type of scales and whether they can be removed properly. Some authorities consider these species acceptable. You will find a useful list of kosher and nonkosher fish at www.kashrut.com and www.kosherquest.org.

Fish don't require soaking or salting and the blood is not forbidden. In addition, ritual slaughter is not required. Under kashruth, fish is neither meat nor dairy, so you can cook it in any cookware and serve it as part of a dairy or meat meal. (Stricter observance based on Talmudic traditions dictates that fish and meat should not be cooked or eaten together and must be served on separate plates.)

Dairy

All milk and milk products—ice cream, yogurt, butter, and the like—that come from a kosher animal are kosher dairy, as are dairy derivatives. Because of the restriction against mixing meat and dairy, packaged dairy products must not contain any meat and packaged meat products must not contain any dairy. It's important to read labels to avoid "hidden" dairy ingredients (such as casein and lactose) in meat items.

As with other rules regarding kashruth, there is some disagreement when it comes to kosher cheese. You might see a label that says "Cholov Yisroel." This label indicates that the milk products used to produce the cheese have been under constant rabbinical supervision. Cholov Yisroel cheeses are the only ones that qualify as kosher in Orthodox communities. Non-Orthodox authorities have no such requirement.

Soft cheeses, such as cottage cheese, should bear a hekhsher that indicates that the cultures, flavorings, and equipment used in production were kosher. Hard cheeses present other issues. Hard cheeses contain rennet, often derived from animal enzymes, that is used to curdle and coagulate milk. Some authorities state that because the rennet has changed sufficiently from its original meat form and because the amount used is insignificant, any hard cheese is permissible. Orthodox rules, on the other hand, permit only those hard cheeses made with kosher rennet, a nondairy product that comes from vegetable or microbial sources.

Pareve

Foods that aren't meat or dairy are called pareve. You can eat these "neutral" foods in any meat or dairy meal. Pareve items include all fruits, vegetables, grains, permitted fish, and eggs. Assuming they contain no dairy or meat ingredients, foods such as bread, cake, cereal, soda, tea, coffee, pasta, and ingredients such as vegetable oil, sugar, flour, nuts, and seeds are pareve.

Fresh fruit (as well as vegetables, grains, eggs, and fish) do not need rabbinic supervision to be kosher, with the exception of the following grape products: wine, wine vinegar, grape juice, soft drinks that include grape juice, and grape jelly. This rule does not apply to fresh grapes or raisins.

WHAT IS HALAL?

Muslims follow dietary laws that are similar to kashruth and are called *halal*, which means "permissible" in Arabic. Because the kosher and halal philosophies both focus on humane treatment of animals used for food and because the procedures used to slaughter animals are so similar, Muslims are permitted to eat kosher meats if and when halal meats are not available. In parts of the country where halal meats and other products are not widely available, many Muslims consume kosher meats and meat products. The following is a general survey of halal dietary laws.

Meat and Poultry

All meats and poultry are allowed except for pork and any carnivorous animal such as cats, rodents, or birds of prey. Any portion of the animal, including the hindquarter, is permissible. Like kosher meat, halal meat must be from a healthy animal and it must not have been given a diet that contains any animal product. Before slaughter, the animal must be allowed food and water. Slaughtering is similar to the kosher procedure, in that a razor-sharp knife is used and the animal is killed with one stroke so that dying is nearly instantaneous. Muslims do not require a trained shochet; any able adult can perform the ritual as long as he or she washes hands and is not sick. A prayer is said over each animal as it is sacrificed. Once the animal has been slaughtered its blood drains on the ground, then the carcass hangs to allow excess blood to spill off. As with kosher, halal prohibits the eating or drinking of blood. Unlike kosher, halal permits eating meat with dairy.

Fish

Halal rules are less precise regarding fish. There are several prevailing opinions based on tradition and commentary. Most Sunni Muslims believe that any life that comes out of the waters may be eaten. Most Shiite Muslims follow a rule closer to kashruth: only fish that have fins and scales are permissible. There is another view that shellfish that live only in the water are allowed (lobster, clam, mussels, and so on) but that marine animals that can live both in and out of the water (crab, turtles, frog) are prohibited.

Food that isn't halal is called *haram,* a word that means "not permissible." Pork and carnivorous animals are haram. Intoxicants of any kind are haram. Observers of halal do not drink beer, liquor, or wine and many adhere to the rule that no intoxicating substance, including alcohol-based ingredients such as vanilla extract, may be used for cooking. On the other hand, some scholars say that the purpose of the law against intoxicating substances has to do with how such substances can overpower the mind. They are of the opinion that the alcohol in extracts and spirits evaporates during cooking and is therefore permissible.

A LAST WORD

All the recipes in this book are kosher. Some of the products used rely on a variety of hekhshers that may not be acceptable to those who follow a stricter tradition of kashruth. As I mentioned in the beginning of this chapter, if you ever have a question about whether a product or particular food is kosher or not, it is always advisable to consult your local authority on halakha.

CULINARY ESSENTIALS FOR THE KOSHER KITCHEN

It's not easy to get dinner on the table every night. But a well-stocked kitchen can be a real help. You may not have room for large numbers of cans and other packaged goods, but storing even a few staples allows you keep shopping time to a minimum, because you'll only have to pick up fresh items like meat or vegetables.

Fortunately kosher home cooks today can choose from a vast array of canned, jarred, and packaged goods certified with a hekhsher, and every year more and more products are approved. Take a look at the enormous variety of foods: Chinese hoisin sauce, Latin arepa flour, Japanese wasabi powder, Tunisian harissa, Mexican chipotle in adobo, and Middle Eastern

17 ⌒

pomegranate paste. These and thousands more make it easier to create tasty, interesting kosher meals.

You know what the obvious staples are: eggs, flour, sugar, salt, black peppercorns, onions, bread crumbs, and so on. I should note here that I always use large eggs and unsalted butter, and suggest you do the same. All the recipes in this book that include eggs are based on that size; when there is an exception it is specifically indicated. Unsalted butter tastes cleaner and fresher. It's healthier, too, and lets you add the amount of salt, if any, that suits your palate.

In addition to the staples, the following are items I always keep on hand. They give me flexibility and open up a world of possibilities when I cook.

PRODUCE

- Lemons: Countless uses, but especially important for vinaigrette dressings and to squeeze onto fish, rice, and baked potatoes.
- Limes: For salsas, relishes, and to sprinkle on fruit.
- Parsley: Adds flavor, bright color, and a vibrant, fresh quality.
- Scallions: Offer a fresh, crisp, oniony bite to salads and stir-fries.
- Vidalia onions: A mild oniony but sweet addition to cooked foods and salads.
- Fresh ginger: A vibrant and flavorful addition to marinades and stir-fries.
- Garlic: For flavor in innumerable fresh and cooked foods. The peeled cloves are fine, but avoid pre-chopped garlic in a jar, because it can taste rancid and bitter. When garlic is chopped the volatile oils that give it its characteristic pungent flavor deteriorate quickly.
- Fresh herbs: Basil, thyme, mint, and rosemary enhance flavor in salads and soups, and fresh and cooked foods.
- Fresh chile peppers: For spicier, more flavorful, and interesting omelets, frittatas, salsas, salads, casseroles, and stir-fries.

REFRIGERATOR AND FREEZER STAPLES

§ Feta cheese: For salads, quiche, and egg dishes.

§ Parmesan cheese: Numerous uses, especially in pasta, quiche, and pizza.

§ Plain yogurt: For soups, sauces, dips, and smoothies.

§ Olives: Particularly Mediterranean varieties, a lively addition to salads, eggs, relishes, salsas, and pasta, fish, and chicken dishes.

§ Mayonnaise: For salads and sandwiches.

§ Dijon mustard: For sandwiches and for flavoring sauces, home-made condiments, salad dressings, and a host of meat, poultry, and fish dishes.

§ Frozen corn kernels and frozen peas: Add to salads, rice, soups, casseroles, eggs, and many meat, poultry, fish, and vegetarian entrées.

§ Frozen spinach: For pie, quiche, and egg dishes.

§ Frozen pizza dough or packaged pre-made pizza crust: For quick pizza dinners.

CUPBOARD ITEMS

§ Hoisin sauce: For Asian-style stir-fries and salads, barbecue sauce, and as a condiment for meats, poultry, and fish.

§ Harissa and/or schug: Add hot, spicy flavor to soups, salad dressings, vegetables, sauces, meat, poultry, and fish entrées. These condiments are similarly robust, with hot chile peppers; the spices and quantities in each are somewhat different. Try both to see which you prefer. There's a recipe for harissa in the Miscellaneous Basics chapter of this book.

§ Sesame oil: Use near the end of cooking to give an intense and fragrant finish for stir-fries, soups, and grilled meats, also for sauces, marinades, and dipping condiments.

§ Canned beans and packaged lentils: For salads or to add to eggs, soup, or pasta. If you have more time to devote to cooking, you might want to buy dried beans, which require soaking and simmering before being used for recipes. Lentils cook so quickly that there's no need to buy the canned kind, which tend to be mushy.

- § Canned tomatoes: For sauce and soup.
- § Pasta, both strings and tubular shapes: For different pasta dishes.
- § Extra virgin olive oil: For salad dressing, sauce, sautés, and general cooking.
- § Red wine vinegar: For vinaigrette, marinades, and general cooking.
- § Balsamic vinegar: For heartier dressings and to drizzle onto grilled meats and fresh ripe fruit such as strawberries and peaches.
- § Soy sauce: For flavoring Asian-style dishes, barbecue sauce, and stir-fries.
- § Stock: chicken, vegetable, and beef for soups and sauces.
- § Coconut milk or soy milk: nondairy alternatives useful for cream soups, sauces, and meat-based dishes.
- § Dried herbs and spices: Jazz up your recipes. The most important ones include basil, cayenne pepper, chile powder, ground cinnamon, ground cumin, curry powder, oregano, paprika, red pepper flakes, rosemary, and thyme.

There are some additional items that I use frequently and always have in my kitchen. I recommend that you cook with them too. They offer a variety of different tastes that will encourage you to be more creative and to experiment with recipes. Branching out with different ingredients will also make your task of cooking more fun, and your meals, even the "experiments," will be a nice surprise for you and your family and friends. You'll find most of these items in a typical supermarket. Exceptions may be pomegranate paste, zatar, and orange flower water, which you may need to seek out in specialty stores, Middle Eastern markets, or online.

OPTIONAL BUT RECOMMENDED ITEMS

- § Rice wine vinegar: Gives a lighter, milder taste to salad dressings.
- § White wine vinegar: For lighter vinaigrettes, especially those to be paired with chicken, fish, pasta, or potato salad.

- Chipotles in adobo: Spicy, hot, and smoky flavored; they boost flavor in soups, sauces, and sandwiches.

- Sambal, chile paste, or chile paste with garlic: Fiery-hot condiments that will jazz up meat marinades, sauces, and dressings.

- Pomegranate paste: Adds a tart flavor to marinades, glazes, and sauces; it also gives a mysteriously fascinating taste to plain vanilla ice cream.

- Tofutti soy cheese: Tastes like real cheese but is pareve, so it can be used with meat.

- Major Grey's chutney: Does wonders as a condiment for meat and is also useful for marinades, sauces, and glazes, especially for poultry.

- Wasabi powder: Wasabi is the greenish condiment served with sushi. Wasabi powder may be pure, dried wasabi but often contains horseradish or mustard. It is a zesty addition to marinades, sauces, and simple foods such as mashed potatoes. Wasabi mayonnaise comes in handy, too, as a spread and for dipping sauces.

- Mirin: A Japanese rice wine similar to sake (but lower in alcohol content) that is used as a flavoring, especially together with soy sauce. It's terrific on fish and asparagus.

- Teriyaki glaze: For glazing fish and meat.

- Panko: Japanese-style bread crumbs that add a satisfying, crunchy coating to fried and oven-baked foods.

- Quinoa: A nutty-flavored grain, a great alternative to rice, pasta, or couscous. It can be made into side dishes, casseroles, and salads.

- Arepa flour: Cornmeal flour, for fabulous, light, savory pancakes.

- Tart shells: Frozen dough or cookie crumb, for quick desserts.

- Zatar: An aromatic spice mixture used to liven up vinaigrettes, sauces, soups, and dips, and as a sprinkle for meats, poultry, vegetables, olives, and grilled or toasted bread.

- Orange flower water: a delightful, pure, fragrant flavoring made with real orange blossoms and used for desserts.

SOUP

Soup is like the postman. Through snow or rain or gloomy cold, it delivers. During the worst of winter, eating a bowl of thick, hot soup is nourishing, like a liquid electric blanket that will make you feel warm and content. When the weather is hazy, hot, and humid you will find refreshment in cold soup. Soup isn't difficult to make and it's one of the most forgiving kind of recipes, flexible enough for substitutions and reinventions.

If you like soup, it's smart to keep some multipurpose pantry "fixings" at hand and to rethink leftovers and items in your refrigerator. If you're making vegetable soup, for example, and don't have broccoli, you can usually substitute another vegetable like green beans or cauliflower. You can replace fresh tomatoes with canned, add frozen corn and peas for extra chunkiness, or throw in a few dried mushrooms to intensify flavor.

Store-bought stock is reliable, even if it isn't as bountifully flavorful as homemade, and these days there is a huge variety to choose from, including chicken, beef, vegetable, and mushroom broths. Dried and canned beans come in handy for some soups and most recipes will be fine whether you use red kidney beans or pintos, white cannellini or black beans. Condiments and other taste enhancers—harissa, lemon, fresh herbs, and such—can help you bring big flavor to soup by adding just a bit. And don't forget about simple garnishes like Pita Crisps (page 225) or Croutons (page 224). Crunchy textural elements like these make most soups even more appealing.

Some of the soup recipes in this section, including Fresh Tomato Soup with Herbed Whipped Cream (page 36), Pea Soup with Mint (page 40), and Pumpkin Bisque with Curry and Pear (page 29), would be good starters to a meal or make a lovely, light lunch dish. Others, like Bean and Pasta Soup (page 30), Tomato Soup with Chickpeas, Chard, and Harissa (page 33), and Triple Fish Chowder (page 34) are more substantial and nourishing enough to be dinner, especially if you serve them with bread or salad.

White Bean Soup with Frizzled Leeks

This is a lush, velvety soup that in the past I made the long way, using dried beans, but I've found that canned beans are just fine and the soup gets done more quickly. The frizzled leeks are a pleasurably crispy contrast, but if you don't have time to make, them Croutons (page 224), Pita Crisps (page 225), or Garlic Toasts (page 225) will also do nicely. And if you don't have a leek, use an onion. Straining the soup gives it a more elegant finish, but when I'm busy I don't take that step.

> 1 tablespoon extra virgin olive oil
> 1 small onion, chopped
> 1 (15-ounce) can white beans, rinsed and drained
> 4 cups vegetable stock
> 1½ teaspoons minced fresh rosemary
> ½ teaspoon fresh thyme leaves
> ½ teaspoon salt, or to taste
> ⅔ cup cream

Heat the olive oil in a soup pot over medium heat. Add the onion and cook for 2–3 minutes or until slightly softened. Add the beans, stock, rosemary, thyme, and salt. Bring to a boil, lower the heat, and simmer for 30 minutes. Puree the ingredients and strain them through a fine sieve if desired. Return the soup to the pan, add the cream, and heat through. Serve the soup topped with crumbled frizzled leeks. Makes 4 servings.

Frizzled Leeks

1 medium leek
2 tablespoons all-purpose flour
Vegetable oil
Salt, to taste
Pinch of cayenne pepper

Make the leeks while the soup cooks: Remove and discard the green part of the leeks. Cut off and discard the root end. Wash the leeks carefully and dry them. Cut the white portion of the leeks into narrow julienne strips. Dredge them in the flour and shake off the excess. Heat 2 inches of vegetable oil in a deep sauté pan (or use a deep fryer) to about 365°F or until a bread crumb sizzles quickly. Immerse the leeks a few at a time and fry for 2–3 minutes or until they are golden brown. Drain on paper towels and sprinkle with salt and a pinch of cayenne pepper.

Frizzled leeks are wonderfully crispy and useful for lots of other dishes. You can make them as a side dish for grilled or roasted meats or poultry or to scatter on top of salad or over a smooth dip such as hummus.

Bread and Tomato Soup

This soup is so thick it is almost not a soup, but more like flavorful, tomatoey soaked bread. This variation of a traditional Italian dish is particularly wonderful in the summer, when you can get garden fresh, ripe tomatoes.

8–10 ounces Italian bread, ciabatta, Tuscan bread, or
other similar artisanal loaf, preferably one day old
½ cup extra virgin olive oil
2 medium garlic cloves, minced
2 teaspoons minced fresh sage leaves
6 large ripe beefsteak-type tomatoes, coarsely chopped
6 cups beef stock
Several sprigs of fresh thyme (or basil leaves)

Cut the bread into slices about ½ inch thick and set aside uncovered. If the bread is very fresh, preheat the oven to 400°F, place the slices on a cookie sheet and bake for 4–6 minutes or until lightly toasted. Set aside. Heat the olive oil in a soup pot over medium heat. Add the garlic and sage and cook for about 30 seconds. Add the bread and toss the ingredients to distribute them evenly. Add the tomatoes and cook for 4–5 minutes. Add the stock and thyme. Bring the soup to a simmer. Cook for about 25–30 minutes or until the bread has absorbed a good deal of the liquid. Remove the thyme sprigs and serve. Makes 4–6 servings.

Roasted Onion and Fennel Soup

This is a thick, smooth soup that you can prepare for a meat dinner by leaving out the cream (though the cream provides a smooth, luxurious quality) or by using a cream substitute. You can roast the vegetables on one day and prepare the rest of the soup a day or two later.

> 1 bulb fennel
> 1 large Spanish onion, peeled and sliced
> 2 tablespoons extra virgin olive oil
> 1 medium all-purpose or Yukon Gold potato, peeled and
>   cut into chunks
> 2 cups vegetable stock
> 1 teaspoon salt, or to taste
> ½ cup half-and-half cream or cream substitute, optional
> Pita Crisps or Garlic Toasts (see page 225), optional

Preheat the oven to 450°F. Remove the stalks and frilly fronds from the fennel. Cut into the bottom core of the fennel bulb to remove as much of the hard, fibrous center as possible. Cut the bulb into slices. Place the onion and fennel slices on a large cookie sheet. Pour the olive oil over the vegetables and toss them to coat all sides. Roast the vegetables for about 30 minutes or until lightly browned, mixing occasionally. Place the potato, roasted vegetables, stock, 2 cups water, and salt in a soup pot and bring to a boil over high heat. Lower the heat and simmer, partially covered, for 25 minutes or until the vegetables have softened. Puree the soup and return it to the pan to reheat. Add the cream, if desired, and cook for a minute or so to reheat. Top each serving with two Pita Crisps or Garlic Toasts if desired. Makes 4–6 servings.

The fennel's small, feathery fronds make a beautiful garnish.

Carrot and Parsnip Soup

Carrots and parsnips are sturdy winter vegetables that soften sensuously and are perfect for mashing to use a base for soup. Both vegetables are also on the sweet side, so they are well partnered with bolder elements such as ginger and cumin. This soup goes well with flatbread or Pita Crisps (page 225). For a dairy meal, you can garnish the soup with a dollop of plain yogurt or dairy sour cream and chives (use vegetable stock).

>   2 tablespoons extra virgin olive oil
>   1 large onion, chopped
>   2 medium garlic cloves, minced
>   1 teaspoon minced fresh ginger
>   ½ pound carrots, peeled and chopped
>   ½ pound parsnips, peeled and chopped
>   1 teaspoon ground cumin
>   ¾ teaspoon ground coriander
>   Salt and freshly ground black pepper, to taste
>   4 cups vegetable stock or chicken stock

Heat the olive oil in a large saucepan over medium heat. Add the onion and cook for 2–3 minutes or until softened. Add the garlic and ginger and cook for another minute. Add the carrots, parsnips, cumin, coriander, and some salt and pepper to taste. Cook for another minute, stirring ingredients. Add the stock and 1 cup water, bring to a simmer, and cook, partially covered, about 25 minutes or until vegetables are tender. Puree the soup and return it to the pan to reheat, or use a hand blender. Makes 4–6 servings.

For extra richness, make this into cream soup: Add some half-and-half cream at the end and heat through (in this case, make the soup with vegetable stock).

Pumpkin Bisque with Curry and Pear

This is one of my favorite soups. The coconut milk makes it rich, thick, and sweet, and tempers the spicy curry and cayenne. I've made the soup using soy milk, and it's tasty that way, too. For a meat meal, use vegetable oil and chicken stock; for a dairy meal use butter and vegetable stock.

> 2 tablespoons butter or vegetable oil
> 1 medium onion, chopped
> 2 ripe pears, peeled, cored and cut into chunks
> 1 (15-ounce) can pumpkin puree
> 1½ teaspoons curry powder
> ⅛ teaspoon cayenne pepper
> Pinch of ground cinnamon
> 4 cups vegetable stock or chicken stock
> 1 cup coconut milk or soy milk
> Salt, to taste
> 2 tablespoons minced fresh chives or ¼ cup toasted
>   coconut

Heat the butter in a large saucepan over medium heat. When the butter has melted and looks foamy, add the onion and cook for 2–3 minutes or until slightly softened. Add the pear chunks, pumpkin puree, curry powder, cayenne pepper, cinnamon, stock, and coconut milk. Mix ingredients thoroughly. Bring to a simmer and cook for 25 minutes. Puree the soup and return it to the pan to heat (or use a hand blender). Season to taste with salt. Serve sprinkled with chives or toasted coconut. Makes 4–6 servings.

Make sure you buy canned pumpkin puree, not pumpkin pie mix. The mix includes spices, the puree is plain and unseasoned. If you use soy milk, be sure it is plain and unsweetened.

Bean and Pasta Soup

This is a quick version of traditional pasta e fagioli. Leave off the Parmesan cheese and it becomes suitable for a meat meal. Add a teaspoon of Harissa (page 228) or schug and see how the flavor changes completely.

3 tablespoons extra virgin olive oil
1 medium onion, chopped
1 large garlic clove, minced
2 carrots, sliced ½ inch thick
2 stalks celery, sliced ½ inch thick
1 (28-ounce) can tomatoes, with liquid
4 cups vegetable stock
3 tablespoons minced fresh basil
2 tablespoons minced fresh parsley
Salt and freshly ground black pepper, to taste
½ cup ditalini or other small tubular pasta
2 (15-ounce) cans red kidney beans, with liquid
Freshly grated Parmesan cheese or 1 teaspoon harissa
    or schug, optional

Heat the olive oil in a soup pot over medium heat. Add the onion, garlic, carrots, and celery and cook for 2 minutes or until softened slightly. Add the tomatoes, stock, basil, parsley, and some salt and pepper to taste. Bring to a boil and simmer partially covered for 20 minutes. Add the pasta and cook for 5 minutes. Add the beans and cook for another 8–10 minutes or until the pasta is tender. Serve the soup sprinkled with freshly grated Parmesan cheese or stir in the harissa or schug, if desired. Makes 6 servings.

California Gazpacho

I've made dozens of versions of this classic summer dish and like this one the best. The lime juice gives it some tang, while the cumin livens it up a bit. Gazpacho can be chunky or a puree. I find the pureed version more satisfying, but if you like a chunkier version, process each of the vegetables separately (because their textures are so different) to the size you prefer.

2 slices firm, home-style white bread, torn into pieces
1 large garlic clove, cut in half
½ medium red onion, peeled and cut into chunks
3 tablespoons extra virgin olive oil
3 medium tomatoes, cut into chunks
1 Kirby cucumber, cut into chunks
½ sweet red bell pepper, seeds and stem removed,
    cut into chunks
1½ cups tomato juice
¼ cup fresh lime juice
2 teaspoons ground cumin
Salt, to taste
Chopped avocado, optional

Place the bread, garlic, onion, and olive oil into a food processor. Process the ingredients until finely chopped and evenly distributed, scraping down the sides of the bowl once or twice. Add ½ cup water and process to blend it in. Add the tomatoes, cucumber, and bell pepper and pulse until the ingredients are pureed. Pour the soup into a large nonreactive bowl and stir in the tomato juice, lime juice, and cumin. Refrigerate for one hour. Season to taste with salt. Serve the soup with the chopped avocado on top, if desired. Makes 4–6 servings.

A Kirby cucumber is short, with a bumpy, light green or greenish-yellow skin that isn't waxed for long-term storage. Because the skin is thin and the seeds are tiny you don't have to peel Kirbys. They can be difficult to find, except in the summer. A good substitute is the English "seedless" cucumber. Regular cucumbers are fine too, but must be peeled and deseeded.

Chilled Cucumber-Avocado Soup

This soup is smooth and velvety, so you can scatter in some Pita Crisps (page 225) or a few Croutons (page 224) for a nice contrasting crunch. A definite benefit is that you can make this soup two days ahead; just keep it well chilled in the fridge. It is an excellent choice to precede Warm Tuna Niçoise Salad (page 50), Bulgur Wheat Salad with Feta Cheese and Dill Dressing (page 53), or Quinoa Salad with Beans, Corn, and Peppers (page 60). For fish meal partners try Broiled Branzini with Tomato-Olive Relish (page 85) or Pepper-Crusted Bluefish with Horseradish Yogurt Sauce (page 94).

> 2 medium cucumbers
> 1 large ripe Hass avocado
> 3 cups plain yogurt
> 1 cup tomato juice
> 2 tablespoons lime juice
> ½ teaspoon ground cumin
> Salt and freshly ground black pepper, to taste
> 1 cup ice water, approximately
> 4 lime slices

Peel the cucumbers and slice them in half lengthwise. Scoop out the seeds. Cut the cucumbers into chunks and place them in a food processor. Process until the cucumbers are finely minced. Peel the avocado and add the flesh to the processor. Process until the mixture is smooth. Add the yogurt, tomato juice, lime juice, and cumin and process until well blended. Refrigerate for at least one hour. Season to taste with salt and pepper. Thin the soup to the desired consistency with ice water. Spoon the soup into individual serving bowls and garnish each with a lime slice. Makes 4 servings.

Tomato Soup with Chickpeas, Chard, and Harissa

This is an easy version of a popular Moroccan soup. It starts out as a mild tomato-vegetable soup but there's a tiny bit of Harissa (page 228) or schug added at the end to spice it up. It can be a meal in itself, served with a salad and bread or followed by eggs.

> 1 bunch Swiss chard
> 2 tablespoons extra virgin olive oil
> 1 medium onion, chopped
> 1 stalk celery with leaves if possible, chopped
> 1 large garlic clove, minced
> 2 tablespoons tomato paste
> 4 cups vegetable stock
> 1 (2-pound, 3-ounce) can tomatoes, with liquid
> ½ cup minced fresh parsley
> ½ cup tubetti or other small pasta
> 1 (15-ounce) can chickpeas (also called garbanzo beans)
> ½–1½ teaspoons harissa or schug
> Salt and freshly ground black pepper, to taste

Wash and drain the chard and discard any thick stems. Tear the chard into pieces and set aside. Heat the olive oil in a soup pot over medium heat. Add the onion and celery and cook for 3–4 minutes or until the vegetables have softened. Add the garlic and cook briefly. Add the tomato paste and stir it into the vegetables. Add the stock, 1 cup water, tomatoes, and parsley. Break up the tomatoes with a wooden or other long-handled spoon. Bring to a boil, lower the heat and simmer for 15 minutes. Add the pasta and chard and cook for 5 minutes. Add the chickpeas and harissa to taste (begin with ½ teaspoon). Stir and simmer for about 5 minutes or until the pasta is tender. Season to taste with salt and pepper. Makes 4–6 servings.

Triple Fish Chowder

Chowders are thick with ingredients and can be filling as a main course for dinner. Certain fish, sole and flounder, for example, are too soft and can flake too easily in soup, making it murky and not as satisfyingly chunky. It's important to use varieties that are firm and hold together: salmon, tuna, tilapia, snapper, haddock, pollack, hake, and cod are good choices. The fish is added last and cooks for only a short time.

3 tablespoons vegetable oil
1 large onion, chopped
1 leek, thoroughly washed and chopped
2 celery stalks, chopped
2 garlic cloves, minced
1 medium-large jalapeño pepper, deseeded and minced
6 cups fish or vegetable stock
⅔ cup uncooked white rice
6 plum tomatoes, chopped
6 ounces firm white fish, such as tilapia, cut into
    1½-inch chunks
6 ounces fresh salmon, cut into 1½-inch chunks
6 ounces fresh tuna, cut into 1½-inch chunks
½ cup frozen peas
½ cup frozen corn kernels
Salt and freshly ground black pepper, to taste

You can make your own fish stock if you wish, for a more seafoody flavor (there are no kosher commercial fish stocks in the market). It isn't difficult but does take time and effort: ask your fishmonger for fish heads and tails, put them in a pot with a carrot, onion, celery stalk, and some seasoning (salt and pepper, fresh dill, thyme, or tarragon) and cover with water. Bring to a boil, lower the heat, and simmer for about 30 minutes. Strain the stock and use it, or freeze it for about one month.

Heat the vegetable oil in a soup pot over medium heat. Add the onion, leek, celery, garlic, and jalapeño pepper. Cook for 3–4 minutes or until the vegetables have softened. Add the stock, rice, and tomatoes and bring to a boil. Lower the heat, cover the pan and cook for 10 minutes. Add the fish, peas, and corn and simmer, covered, for 10 minutes. Taste for seasoning and add salt and pepper to taste. Makes 4–6 servings.

Sweet-and-Sour Beet Soup

This is a lovely magenta-colored soup, slightly sour, slightly sweet. It's a wonder when served chilled, but in my family we sometimes eat it at room temperature or even slightly warmed. If you want to taste the soup warm, heat it gently after you add the yogurt—don't let the soup come to a boil because it might separate. This soup is a particularly good recipe for a fish meal, including Mackerel Fillets with Lime-Mustard Butter and Scallions (page 86), Roasted Haddock with Tangerine-Paprika Panko Crust (page 96), or Pepper-crusted Bluefish with Horseradish Yogurt Sauce (page 94).

> 1 bunch (about 1 pound) beets
> 1½ teaspoons sugar
> ½ teaspoon salt
> ¼ teaspoon ground coriander
> Freshly ground black pepper, to taste
> 3 tablespoons lemon juice
> 1 cup plain yogurt or buttermilk
> 1 tablespoon minced fresh dill
> 2 medium scallions, minced

Peel the beets and shred them in a food processor. Place the beets and 3 cups water in a large saucepan and bring to a boil over high heat. Lower the heat and add the sugar, salt, coriander, and pepper. Cover the pan and simmer for 20 minutes. Add the lemon juice and simmer, uncovered, for 10 minutes. Chill the soup. Stir in the yogurt or buttermilk. Top each serving of soup with a sprinkling of fresh dill and scallion. Makes 4 servings.

Wear rubber or disposable gloves when you peel beets to protect your fingers and hands from becoming stained.

Don't throw away the beet greens! They are a wonderful side dish (see the recipe for Beet Greens with Red Onions and Raisins on page 188).

Fresh Tomato Soup with Herbed Whipped Cream

This recipe involves peeling fresh tomatoes and squeezing out the seeds, so it is a little more involved than most of the other recipes in this book, but it means the soup will be smooth and luxurious. The whipped cream garnish gives the soup a pretty finish and extra-rich flavor, but if you're looking to cut fat from your diet you can substitute yogurt (nonfat is fine).

6 large ripe tomatoes
2 tablespoons extra virgin olive oil
1 tablespoon butter
1 medium onion, chopped
Salt and freshly ground black pepper, to taste
2 tablespoons minced fresh basil
2 teaspoons minced fresh oregano
3 cups vegetable stock
¾ cup light cream or half-and-half cream
½ cup whipping cream, whipped until stiff
2 teaspoons minced fresh herbs

Bring a large pot of water to a boil. Immerse the tomatoes for 20 seconds, then drain them under cold water. Peel the tomatoes, remove the stems, and cut the tomatoes in half crosswise. Squeeze out the seeds. Chop the tomatoes and set them aside. Heat the olive oil and butter in a soup pot over medium heat. When the butter has melted and looks foamy, add the onion and cook for 2–3 minutes or until the pieces have softened. Add the tomatoes, salt, pepper, basil, and oregano. Cover the pan and cook the vegetables for 15 minutes. Add about ½ cup of the stock to the vegetables and puree the vegetables in a blender or food processor (or use a hand blender). Return the ingredients to the saucepan. Stir in the remaining stock and bring the soup to a simmer. Cook for 5–6 minutes. Stir in the cream and heat through. Serve with a dollop of whipped cream mixed with herbs. Makes 4 servings.

Hungarian Mushroom Soup

The recipe for this creamy and aromatic soup was given to me by Judith Roll and Rebecca Martin, who operate the Sweet On You Bakery & Café at the JCC in Stamford, Connecticut. Like many dishes of Hungarian origin, it has a considerable amount of paprika, making it rich and hearty, with a gorgeous autumn orange color.

6 tablespoons butter
1 small onion, minced
10 ounces white mushrooms, sliced
10 ounces portobello mushrooms, chopped
3 large garlic cloves, minced
2 tablespoons paprika
¼ cup all-purpose flour
4 cups vegetable stock
1 cup whole milk
1 tablespoon soy sauce
2 tablespoons minced fresh dill
¾ cup dairy sour cream
1½ teaspoons lemon juice
Salt and freshly ground black pepper, to taste

Place the butter in a soup pot over medium heat. When the butter has melted and looks foamy, add the onion and mushrooms and cook for about 8 minutes. Add the garlic and paprika and stir for 1 minute, until combined. Stir in the flour and mix continuously for 3 minutes. Gradually add the stock and milk, stirring until combined. Add the soy sauce and dill. Raise the heat and bring the liquid to a boil. Lower the heat and simmer for 20 minutes. Stir in the dairy sour cream, lemon juice, and salt and pepper to taste. Makes 4 servings.

Wash mushrooms under cold water with the cap up, gills down. This keeps them from becoming soggy and waterlogged. If there's dirt in the gills, rinse the mushrooms on both sides and dry them quickly with paper towels.

Lentil Soup with Cheese

This is a thick, chunky, rib-sticking soup. The cheese melts into the liquid and provides even more body to the dish. The texture is best when you puree a portion of the soup, so I've recommended it, but it's perfectly fine if you don't want to bother with that step. Warm pita or whole-grain bread would be a good accompaniment.

2 tablespoons extra virgin olive oil
1 medium onion, chopped
2 tablespoons minced fresh parsley
1 tablespoon minced fresh dill
6 cups vegetable stock
1 cup lentils
1 tablespoon apple cider vinegar
1 cup corn kernels
Salt and freshly ground black pepper, to taste
1½ to 2 cups shredded cheddar cheese

Heat the olive oil in a soup pot over medium heat. Add the onion and cook for 3–4 minutes or until softened. Add the parsley, dill, and stock and bring the liquid to a boil. Lower the heat and add the lentils. Cover the pot and simmer for 20–25 minutes or until the lentils are tender. Add the vinegar and cook for another 2–3 minutes. Remove 3 cups of the soup and puree in a blender or food processor (or use a hand blender). Return the ingredients to the pan. Add the corn. Cook for 3–4 minutes. Season to taste with salt and pepper. Serve the soup with the shredded cheese on top. Makes 4–6 servings.

Turkey Meatball Soup with Egg and Spinach

I've made this tangy soup without the meatballs and it's wonderful as a first course. Add the meat and it's hearty and satisfying enough for dinner. When I don't include the meat I sometimes use vegetable stock, making it fine as a first course for a dairy dinner.

16–20 ounces ground turkey
1 small onion, minced
2 tablespoons minced fresh mint
2 tablespoons minced fresh dill
½ teaspoon finely grated fresh lemon peel
All-purpose flour for dredging, plus 1 tablespoon
8 cups chicken stock
½ cup white rice
1 pound spinach, washed and coarsely cut
3 tablespoons lemon juice
2 large eggs
Salt and freshly ground black pepper, to taste

Place the ground turkey, onion, mint, dill, and lemon peel in a bowl and mix the ingredients gently to distribute them evenly. Shape the meat into small (1-inch) balls. Roll the balls in flour to coat the surfaces. Set aside. Heat the chicken stock to a simmer in a soup pot over medium heat. Add the rice and drop in the turkey meatballs. Cook, covered, for 12–15 minutes or until the rice is tender but still firm. Add the spinach and cook for 2 minutes. Mix the 1 tablespoon flour and lemon juice until smooth. Add the eggs to the flour mixture and beat the ingredients until smooth and thoroughly blended. Gradually add ½ cup of the hot soup to the egg mixture. Pour the egg mixture into the soup and cook, stirring gently once or twice, for 2–3 minutes or until the soup thickens. Season to taste with salt and pepper. Makes 4–6 servings.

Pea Soup with Mint

This beautiful spring green soup can start dinner or be served for lunch, followed by a sandwich or salad. The soup is more elegant and refined if you strain it but I rarely do that. It tastes the same either way. Fresh peas are always recommended but they aren't always available often or for long—usually just in the late spring or early summer. Most of the time I use the frozen kind.

> 1 tablespoon extra virgin olive oil
> 1 tablespoon butter
> 2 medium scallions, chopped
> 2 teaspoons minced fresh ginger
> 1 (1- by ½-inch) piece lemon peel
> 4 cups vegetable stock
> 2 (10-ounce) packages thawed frozen peas
>   (or use fresh peas)
> ½ cup coarsely chopped fresh mint
> ½ cup plain yogurt
> Salt and freshly ground black pepper, to taste
> Pita Crisps (page 225) or Croutons (page 224)

Heat the olive oil and butter in a large saucepan over medium heat. When the butter has melted and looks foamy, add the scallions and ginger and cook for 2–3 minutes or until softened. Add the lemon peel and stock, bring to a simmer, cover the pan, and cook for 10 minutes. Add the peas and mint and cook uncovered for 5 minutes. Discard the lemon peel. Puree the ingredients in a blender or food processor (or use a hand blender) and strain through a large-holed sieve if desired. Chill thoroughly. Whisk in the yogurt. Season to taste with salt and pepper. Serve with Pita Crisps or Croutons. Makes 4 servings.

SALADS

Salads have had their ups and downs over the centuries. They were stylish in ancient Rome but by the Middle Ages no one knew what a salad was. Then, when England's Queen Elizabeth I came to power in 1558 they came back into fashion.

Things were no different in America. Thomas Jefferson may have loved greens and vinaigrette, but for the most part Americans thought of the stuff as something to avoid. Just a few generations ago, they called it "rabbit food." Men thought of salad as food fit only for ladies' luncheons.

That salads have come and gone on the culinary scene is a good example of how foods and cooking styles are, like most things, subject to the whims of fashion. Today, salads are popular partly because they can be healthy. Assuming you don't load it down with fat-laden, high-calorie dressings, a salad is a friend to anyone who cares about cholesterol, fat, and weight gain. Isn't that all of us?

There's no denying that salads are also well received because they're so versatile. You can create a salad using only greens like lettuce, arugula, and spinach, or with vegetables, meats, or fish, grains or pasta. Or fruit.

You can start a salad from scratch or make one out of leftovers. There are salads (like Tomato Salad with Toasted Bread and Feta Cheese, page 55) that are better suited to a first course or light lunch, but others, including Warm Tuna Niçoise Salad (page 50) and Steak Salad with Mustard-Shallot Vinaigrette (page 48), are substantial enough for dinner. Fresh fruit salads like Grapefruit and Orange Salad with Mint Dressing (page 64) are serviceable as an appetizer but also contain just enough natural sugar to satisfy a sweet tooth at the end of a meal. Because salads are so flexible, they, are a definite advantage for the kosher cook. Those that contain dairy are limited to dairy meals, those with meat, to meat meals. But so many are pareve, containing only greens, vegetables, legumes, grains, or fruit, that they are appropriate for meat or dairy meals.

The recipes I've chosen include salads of all types, all with individual, freshly prepared dressing. Homemade dressings are more flavorful than bottled ones and don't contain additives, preservatives, sugars, and stabilizers. I rarely follow the old-fashioned formula for vinaigrette (3 or 4 to 1 ratio of salad oil to vinegar). Instead, I use more vinegar or other acidic ingredients because they gives a salad more taste with fewer calories.

With the exception of salads consisting mostly of lettuces and greens, most fresh salads are better after they've rested for about 15 minutes after preparation when the flavors of the dressing and other ingredients have time to blend and mellow. Salads also taste best when they are at room temperature, warm, or slightly chilled (there are hot salads, too). Cold masks flavor so don't serve a salad straight from the refrigerator. If you've done the preparation in advance, let the salad stand at room temperature for about a half-hour before you plan to serve it.

MEAT, POULTRY,
AND FISH SALADS

Chicken and Sugar Snap Salad
with Hoisin Vinaigrette

This is a good way to use leftover chicken. Mild chicken meat is a great foil for flavorful condiments like hoisin sauce and vinaigrette dressing. You can serve this salad warm or at room temperature.

4 cups cut-up cooked chicken
5 tablespoons vegetable oil
1 tablespoon chopped fresh ginger
6 thick scallions, chopped
2 cups cut-up shiitake mushroom caps
2 cups cut-up sugar snap peas
2 tablespoons hoisin sauce
2 tablespoons rice wine vinegar or white vinegar
1 tablespoon soy sauce
1 teaspoon sesame oil
Red pepper flakes, optional
1 tablespoon sesame seeds, toasted

Place the chicken in a bowl. Heat 2 tablespoons vegetable oil in a sauté pan. Add the ginger, scallions, mushrooms, and sugar snap peas. Cook for about 2 minutes or until the vegetables are slightly wilted but still crispy. Remove from the pan and add to the chicken. Combine the hoisin sauce, vinegar, remaining 3 tablespoons vegetable oil, soy sauce, and sesame oil and mix thoroughly until well combined. Pour the dressing over the chicken and vegetables. Sprinkle with red pepper flakes if desired. Toss the ingredients again and sprinkle the sesame seeds on top. Makes 4 servings.

Turkey Couscous Salad with Grapes, Oranges, and Cashews

This light dish is wonderful in the summer but it also works after Thanksgiving when you're looking for a good, not too filling way to use leftover turkey. Like many of the recipes I love, this one can be changed to suit your fancy—make it with chicken or use almonds or pistachios instead of cashews. The grapes, oranges, and red onion give the dish a lot of color, so consider this recipe if you're serving buffet style.

> 1¼ cups chicken stock
> 1 cup couscous
> ¾ cup broken cashews
> 1 pound cooked turkey, chopped into ½-inch pieces
> 1 cup red seedless grapes, cut in half
> 2 navel oranges
> ½ cup chopped red onion
> ¼ cup minced fresh parsley, preferably flat leaf
> 6 tablespoons extra virgin olive oil
> ¼ cup orange juice
> ¼ cup lemon juice
> Salt and freshly ground black pepper, to taste

Preheat the oven or toaster oven to 400°F. Bring the stock to a boil and stir in the couscous. Remove from the heat, cover the pan, and let stand for 5 minutes. Fluff the couscous with a fork and spoon it into a bowl. Spread the cashews on a baking sheet and toast in the oven for about 5–8 minutes or until they are fragrant and lightly browned. Add the turkey, grapes, and nuts to the couscous. Peel the oranges, cut them into thick slices and trim the white pith from around the edges. Cut the oranges into segments and add to the bowl. Add the red onion and parsley. Toss ingredients gently. Combine the olive oil, orange juice, and lemon juice, whisk vigorously, and pour over the salad. Toss the ingredients again and season to taste with salt and pepper. Makes 4 servings.

Nuts keep better and taste fresher if you store them in the freezer. Pack them in small plastic freezer bags.

Chicken Waldorf Salad with Dates
and Caramelized Pistachio Nuts

Waldorf salad is a classic American dish that has been on the culinary scene since its invention—not by a chef but by Oscar Tschirky, a maître d'hotel of New York's Waldorf-Astoria in March of 1896. The original salad consisted solely of apples and celery mixed with mayonnaise, but soon after its invention cooks added walnuts and thus the recipe stood for about one hundred years. Today, Waldorf salad comes in many guises and is the kind of recipe that cries out for innovative touches. I add chicken, to turn it into a more substantial lunch or dinner salad, and I've nixed the walnuts in favor of caramelized pistachios because I like their crunch and sweetness next to the soft meat. Because we love dates in our family, I also include some dates, but sometimes I substitute dried cranberries or raisins.

> 2 tablespoons sugar
> 2 teaspoons balsamic vinegar
> ½ cup pistachios
> 3 cups diced cooked chicken
> 1 tart apple, peeled and chopped
> ½ cup chopped dates
> ½ cup mayonnaise
> 1 tablespoon lime juice
> 1½ tablespoons minced fresh tarragon

Preheat the oven to 325°F. Spray a small baking dish with nonstick spray. Combine the sugar and vinegar in small saucepan. Cook over medium heat until the sugar dissolves, about 2 minutes. Add the nuts and toss to coat them completely. Place the nuts on the sprayed baking dish. Bake for 10 minutes or until they are browned and toasty. Cool completely and break the nuts apart. Set aside. In a bowl, combine the chicken, apple, and dates. In another bowl, mix the mayonnaise, lime juice, and tarragon. Spoon the mayonnaise mixture over the chicken and toss to coat all the ingredients. Sprinkle the salad with the nuts. Makes 4 servings.

If there's no time to make the caramelized pistachios, substitute toasted almonds or walnuts.

Orzo Salad with Chicken and Mango

Orange peel and cloves infuse a spicy-citrusy quality to this salad. It's a particularly refreshing dish that I have served many times and have used for parties. Sometimes I mix in dried blueberries or cranberries. If you use dried blueberries, let them soak for about 15 minutes to plump them up.

> 6 tablespoons extra virgin olive oil
> Peel of one orange (in strips)
> 8 whole cloves
> 2 cups orzo pasta
> 3–4 cups cut-up cooked chicken
> ½ cup dried raisins or currants
> 1 mango, peeled and chopped
> 2 tablespoons minced fresh cilantro
> ¼ cup lime juice
> Salt and freshly ground black pepper, to taste

Place the olive oil, orange peel, and cloves in a saucepan and cook over medium heat for about 5 minutes. Set aside to cool. When cool, remove and discard the orange peel and cloves. Cook the orzo according to package directions, drain the pasta, and put it in a bowl. Add the chicken, raisins, mango, and cilantro and toss the ingredients. Pour in the flavored olive oil and lime juice and toss the ingredients again. Season to taste with salt and pepper. Makes 4–6 servings.

Salmon Cobb Salad

Every home cook knows how satisfying it is to put together a terrific-tasting dish in almost no time, using whatever you have on hand in your pantry and fridge. Most often these recipes are never-to-be-repeated spur-of-the-moment flashes of genius, but every once in a while one of them becomes the family's favorite slap-dash dinner, the one you return to and refine over time as the items in your pantry may vary. That's precisely the story of cobb salad. It was invented on a whim and became an American classic. Official legend has it that this famous dish came about in 1937 when Bob Cobb, then the owner of Hollywood's renowned Brown

Derby Restaurant, was about to prepare dinner and looked for inspiration inside the refrigerator. He pulled out a little of this, a little of that, and put together a dish that became an immediate hit. This is obviously a recipe you can change over and over. Our family likes it with leftover salmon because it makes the salad light and refreshing, but filling enough to satisfy.

1 head romaine lettuce
4 cups grilled, broiled, or poached salmon, chopped
1 (15 ounce) can chickpeas, drained and rinsed
1 large cucumber, peeled, deseeded, and chopped
2 tomatoes, chopped
1 small green bell pepper, chopped
½ cup chopped scallion
4 hard-cooked eggs, chopped
1 cup crumbled feta cheese
½ cup chopped black olives
¼ cup minced fresh dill
½ cup extra virgin olive oil
6 tablespoons fresh lemon juice
Freshly ground black pepper, to taste
Pita bread

Wash and dry the lettuce leaves and break them into smaller pieces. Place the leaves on a large platter. Arrange the salmon, chickpeas, cucumber, tomatoes, green pepper, scallion, eggs, feta cheese, and black olives on top. Sprinkle the salad with the chopped dill. Mix the olive oil and lemon juice and pour over the salad. Season with pepper to taste. Serve with pita bread. Makes 4–6 servings.

Cobb salad is one of a number of "composed salads" that are prepared with a variety of ingredients that are arranged neatly on a platter rather than being tossed. For the prettiest effect in this one, place dark items like black olives next to bright ones (feta or eggs). Composed salads often contain protein as well as produce, so they can be filling enough as a main course salad.

Steak Salad with Mustard-Shallot Vinaigrette

This is a terrific dinner dish but I also like to serve this salad when I have a party because it looks so pretty and everything can be made ahead and placed on a platter (if you do this don't dress the salad until just before serving time). Even people who say they don't usually eat red meat gobble this up.

1½ pounds boneless beef steak
1 head romaine lettuce
2 dozen olives
2 large tomatoes, cut up
12–16 cooked asparagus spears, cut into 1½-inch pieces
½ cup extra virgin olive oil or vegetable oil
¼ cup red wine vinegar
1 tablespoon Dijon mustard
1 large shallot, finely chopped
1 teaspoon fresh thyme leaves
Freshly ground black pepper, to taste

Preheat the oven broiler or outdoor grill with the rack about 6 inches from the heat source. Place the beef on a cooking tray and cook for about 3–4 minutes per side or until cooked to the desired doneness. Let rest for 10 minutes before slicing. Wash and dry the lettuce leaves and break them into smaller pieces. Place the lettuce on each of four plates. Scatter the olives, tomatoes, and asparagus around the lettuce. Slice the meat and place equal amounts of it on each plate on top of the vegetables. Combine the olive oil, red wine vinegar, Dijon mustard, shallot, and thyme in a bowl and whisk them together until well blended. Pour the dressing over the salad. Season to taste with pepper. Makes 4 servings.

This is another accommodating dish that you can change to suit your particular needs. Add a few cut-up cooked potatoes, hard-cooked eggs, or some cooked pasta spirals if you like. Or substitute grilled boneless lamb for the beef—in that case, you might want to include cooked white beans in the dish (use a one-pound can and don't forget to rinse them). Or switch to chicken, but cut down on the amount of mustard used in the dressing.

Warm Lentil Salad with Sausage

I used to make plain lentil salad often. One day I bought some chicken-turkey sausage and added it to my tried-and-true recipe and everyone loved the result. Without the meat this is a suitable side dish for any kind of meal. It is also a tasty and texturally satisfying "bed" for roasted or grilled salmon or other meaty fish. With the crispy bits of sausage, it's dinner.

2 cups lentils
1 bay leaf
4 cups cold water, chicken stock, or vegetable stock
⅓ cup plus 2 tablespoons extra virgin olive oil
1 pound chicken or turkey sausage, cut into small pieces
1 medium onion, chopped
2 garlic cloves, minced
1 cup diced zucchini
2 large tomatoes, chopped
⅓ cup red wine vinegar
1½ tablespoons Dijon mustard
1½ teaspoons fresh thyme leaves
Salt and freshly ground black pepper, to taste

Rinse the lentils and place them in a large saucepan with the bay leaf and water or stock. Bring to a boil over high heat, lower the heat, and simmer, partially covered, for about 20–25 minutes or until the lentils are tender. Discard the bay leaf. Drain the lentils and spoon them into a bowl. Let cool slightly. While the lentils are cooking, heat 1 tablespoon olive oil in a nonstick skillet over medium heat and fry the sausage for 6–8 minutes, or until crispy. Stir the sausage occasionally to brown all sides. Add 1 tablespoon olive oil to the pan. Add the onion and cook for 2 minutes. Add the garlic and zucchini and cook for 1 minute. Transfer the ingredients to the bowl with the lentils. Add the tomatoes. Toss ingredients gently. Let stand for about 5 minutes. Whisk together the remaining ⅓ cup olive oil, vinegar, Dijon mustard, and thyme. Pour the dressing over the salad and toss gently. Season to taste with salt and pepper. Makes 4 servings.

This salad is best when served warm. However, you can make it in advance and keep it in the refrigerator. Remove the salad about a half-hour before serving time. Because the lentils will absorb some of the dressing as it sits, the salad may seem too dry, so it might be necessary to add some extra olive oil or vinegar.

Warm Tuna Niçoise Salad

Niçoise salad is a classic French specialty that is also popular in the United States. It's often made with canned tuna, but this version uses fresh, grilled tuna steaks. I also prefer edamame, because of its high protein and antioxidant value, to the more typical green beans, but either will do.

> 4 (6–8 ounce) tuna steaks, 1¼ inch thick
> ½ cup extra virgin olive oil, plus 1 tablespoon for
>   brushing tuna
> 12 small new potatoes
> 1 cup fresh or frozen edamame (or use 2 cups
>   cut-up green beans)
> ¼ cup red wine vinegar or lemon juice
> 1 teaspoon Dijon mustard
> Salt and freshly ground black pepper, to taste
> 2 teaspoons minced fresh thyme, marjoram, or oregano
>   (or a mixture of herbs)
> Oak leaf, Boston, or Bibb lettuce, rinsed and dried
> 8 radicchio leaves, rinsed and dried
> 2 tomatoes, cut into wedges
> ½ cup black olives
> 4 hard-cooked eggs, cut into 4 wedges
> Bell pepper pieces, optional
> Croutons (page 224) or Garlic Toasts (page 225), optional

Preheat an outdoor grill or oven broiler with the rack about 4–6 inches from the heat source (or use a grill pan). Brush the tuna with a film of olive oil. Cook the fish for about 3 minutes per side. The fish should be rare. Remove the fish from the heat to a cutting board. Place the potatoes in a saucepan and cover with water. Bring to a boil and simmer for about 15 minutes or until they are tender. Drain the potatoes and cut them into bite-size pieces when they are cool enough to handle. Set aside. Cook the fresh edamame in simmering water for 3–4 minutes or until tender (or thaw the frozen edamame or cook green beans in simmering water for about 4 minutes or until tender). Drain and set aside. To make the dressing, combine ½ cup olive oil, vinegar, mustard, salt, pepper, and thyme, mix well, and set aside. Line 4 plates with a few lettuce leaves and radicchio. Slice the fish and place the slices on the lettuce. Arrange the potatoes, edamame, tomatoes, olives, egg wedges, bell pepper pieces, and croutons, if used, attractively on each plate. Mix the salad dressing ingredients briefly and pour over the salad. Makes 4 servings.

You can switch to traditional canned tuna if you prefer—use one 6-ounce can per person. That may sound like a lot, and most recipes call for 2–3 ounces per person. But as a main course for dinner 6 ounces is more likely to be satisfying.

White Bean Salad with Grilled Salmon and Lemon-Tarragon Dressing

This is a variation on traditional Tuscan white bean salad. It's among the easiest dishes to make, so it is a real boon on a very busy day.

> 1 pound fresh salmon
> 6 tablespoons extra virgin olive oil, plus 1 tablespoon for
> brushing salmon
> 1 (15-ounce) can white beans, rinsed and drained
> ½ cup chopped red onion
> ½ cup thawed frozen peas
> 3 tablespoons lemon juice
> 1 teaspoon Dijon mustard
> 1½ tablespoons minced fresh tarragon
> Salt and freshly ground black pepper, to taste

Preheat an outdoor grill or oven broiler with the rack about 4–6 inches from the heat source (or use a grill pan). Brush the salmon with a film of olive oil. Cook the fish for about 10 minutes or until cooked to the desired doneness. Let cool. Cut the salmon into smaller pieces. Combine the beans, salmon, onion, and peas in a bowl. Mix 6 tablespoons olive oil, lemon juice, mustard, and tarragon and pour over the salad. Toss gently and season to taste with salt and pepper. Makes 4 servings.

There are several kinds of canned white beans: Great Northern, navy, and cannellini. Any will do for this recipe. Chickpeas are even fine, too.

VEGETABLE, GRAIN, AND FRUIT SALADS

Asparagus Salad with Toasted Almonds and Goat Cheese

This refreshing salad is perfect as a first course at a vegetarian dinner or as an accompaniment to smoked fish. It's also quite versatile: change the cheese to feta, the almonds to walnuts or cashews, and see how the flavor changes!

¼ cup chopped almonds
1 pound medium asparagus spears
2 tablespoons chopped shallot
1½ teaspoons minced fresh mint
1½ teaspoons minced fresh dill
3 tablespoons extra virgin olive oil
2 tablespoons white wine vinegar
Salt and freshly ground black pepper, to taste
2 ounces crumbled goat cheese

Preheat the oven to 400°F. Place the almonds on a cookie sheet and bake them for about 5–8 minutes or until lightly toasted. Remove from the oven and let cool. While the nuts are baking, wash the asparagus and cut off the tough, woody ends. Place the asparagus in a pan, add 1 cup of water, cover the pan, bring the water to a boil, and cook over high heat for 4–6 minutes or until tender, but still crispy. Drain under cold water, wipe dry, and cut into bite-size chunks. Place the asparagus in a bowl. Add the almonds, shallot, mint, and dill. Pour in the olive oil and vinegar and toss ingredients to coat with the dressing. Season to taste with salt and pepper. Spoon onto plates. Top with crumbled cheese. Makes 4 servings.

Bulgur Wheat Salad
with Feta Cheese and Dill Dressing

This dish is like a cross between tabbouleh and Israeli salad, which is a refreshing combination of chopped vegetables, typically tomatoes, cucumbers, and sometimes bell peppers. It's perfect for a dairy dinner, but you could also eat this for breakfast, adding toasted pita bread, on a hot summer day. Leave out the cheese and it becomes suitable for a meat meal.

1 cup fine-grain bulgur wheat
1 cup cut-up cherry tomatoes
1 cup thawed frozen peas
1 medium cucumber, peeled, deseeded, and chopped
¾ cup crumbled feta or blue cheese
¼ cup minced fresh dill
¼ cup extra virgin olive oil
3–4 tablespoons lemon juice, to taste
Salt and freshly ground black pepper, to taste

Place the bulgur wheat in a bowl and pour in 1½ cups boiling water. Stir and let stand for about 15 minutes, or until the wheat is tender. If any liquid remains, strain the wheat to discard the excess. Place the wheat in a bowl. Add the tomatoes, peas, cucumber, cheese, and dill and toss ingredients. Mix the olive oil and lemon juice together and pour over the salad. Toss to coat ingredients with the dressing. Season to taste with salt and pepper. Makes 4–6 servings.

Farro Salad with Grape Tomatoes, Green Beans, and Sweet Onions

Farro is an ancient grain—archaeologists have found it in ancient Egyptian tombs! But it has become trendy, modern fare these days. It's a type of wheat (some call it Emmer wheat) and has a pleasantly chewy texture and nutty flavor. Like other whole grains, it's a good choice to add to soups or use as a base for salads. This recipe is very adaptable. You can add sautéed wild mushrooms or soaked dried porcinis, or cooked vegetables like peas and corn. Farro is now available in many supermarkets (usually in rice and pasta aisle) and in health food stores, but if you can't find it, make this salad using barley.

1½ cups semi-pearled farro
1 cup cut-up green beans
1 cup halved grape tomatoes
1 cup chopped Vidalia or other sweet onion
¼ cup minced parsley
¼ cup extra virgin olive oil
3 tablespoons red wine vinegar or lemon juice
1 teaspoon Dijon mustard
Salt and freshly ground black pepper, to taste

Place the farro in a saucepan and add enough water to cover by one inch. Bring the water to a boil over high heat. Lower the heat, cover the pan, and simmer for about 30 minutes or until the farro is tender. Drain the farro if any liquid remains and place it in a bowl. Let cool slightly. While the farro is cooking, place the green beans in a small amount of water in a saucepan, bring to a boil over high heat, lower the heat, cover the pan and cook for 4–5 minutes or until tender. Rinse the beans under cold water and drain them. Add to the cooked farro. Add the tomatoes, onion, and parsley. Toss ingredients. In a small bowl combine the olive oil, vinegar and mustard. Pour over the salad and toss ingredients. Season to taste with salt and pepper. Makes 4–6 servings.

> Many people soak farro overnight and cook it for an hour or more, but this makes the grain mushy. Farro is best when it is slightly chewy and resilient.

Tomato Salad
with Toasted Bread and Feta Cheese

This hearty, substantial take on traditional panzanella salad is a wonderful way to use fabulous fresh summer tomatoes. The dish can stand alone as a meal, but it's also a good partner for other salads and grain dishes. Or leave out the feta and use it for a meat meal. Crisping the bread prevents it from becoming overly soggy when mixed with the juicy tomatoes and the dressing. Happily, even when it sits for a while and the bread absorbs the liquid, this salad is still quite delicious.

6 slices baguette bread, cut 1½ inches thick
6 tablespoons extra virgin olive oil
4 medium ripe summer tomatoes, cut up
8 ounces feta cheese, crumbled
¼ cup chopped red onion
3 tablespoons minced fresh parsley
1½ tablespoons minced fresh dill
3–4 tablespoons red wine vinegar or lemon juice
½ teaspoon Dijon mustard
Freshly ground black pepper, to taste

Lightly brush the bread on the cut sides with olive oil, using about 1½ tablespoons. Toast the bread in a toaster oven or grill it on an outdoor grill for 2–3 minutes per side, or until crispy and lightly browned. Cut the bread into quarters, place in a bowl and set aside. Add the tomatoes, feta cheese, red onion, parsley, and dill and toss ingredients. In a small bowl, whisk the remaining 4½ tablespoons olive oil, 3 tablespoons vinegar, and the mustard. Pour the dressing over the salad. Toss and let macerate for at least 5 minutes before serving. Taste for seasoning and add more vinegar if desired. Season to taste with pepper. Makes 4 servings.

Cucumber Salad

There's an excellent reason for the expression "cool as a cucumber." Cucumbers are about 96 percent water so they are always thirst quenching and rejuvenating, and not even the harshest heat wave can quell their ability to refresh. They are amazingly low in calories, too, which makes this salad, prepared with lowfat yogurt, a winner whatever the season.

2 large cucumbers, peeled and sliced
1 small Vidalia onion, sliced
½ cup white wine vinegar
¼ cup plain lowfat yogurt
1 tablespoon brown sugar
1 teaspoon salt
1 tablespoon minced fresh cilantro
4 dried red chile peppers

Place the cucumbers and onion in a bowl. Mix the vinegar, yogurt, sugar, and salt and pour over the vegetables. Sprinkle with the cilantro. Break the chile peppers in half, remove the seeds, and scatter the pods over the cucumbers. Toss the ingredients gently. Let marinate for at least one hour. Serve at room temperature or slightly chilled. Makes 6 servings.

Coleslaw with Raisins

No matter how many new and trendy salad recipes you can concoct, no matter how many treasured old salad recipes you can collect, few surpass coleslaw for pure refreshment. Coleslaw is an American staple. We learned to make it first from the Dutch, who called it *koolsla* (cabbage salad). We think of it as shredded cabbage with a mayo dressing and that's how you'll find it in many delis. But I think there are as many recipes for coleslaw as there are people. This version is colorful because of the shredded snow peas and carrots. Raisins add a hint of sweetness. The mayo dressing is light because it's mixed with yogurt. If you want to serve this dish with a meat meal, substitute more mayonnaise for the yogurt.

3 cups shredded green cabbage
2 shredded carrots
18 snow peas, cut lengthwise into narrow shreds
2 thick scallions, chopped
½ cup raisins
¼ cup plain yogurt
¼ cup mayonnaise
1 tablespoon apple cider vinegar
1 teaspoon Dijon mustard
Salt and freshly ground black pepper, to taste

Place the shredded cabbage, carrots, and snow peas in a bowl. Add the scallions and raisins. Toss the ingredients. In another bowl, mix the yogurt, mayonnaise, vinegar, and mustard. Spoon the dressing over the vegetables and toss to coat them completely. Season to taste with salt and pepper. Makes 4 servings.

Chopped Salad with Feta Cheese, Chickpeas, and Zatar Vinaigrette

Chopped salad is a quick fix for any meal, including breakfast. Turn it into a sandwich by stuffing it into a pita pocket. The dressing for this salad contains zatar, an aromatic spice mixture popular in the Middle East. You can find it at many supermarkets and specialty food stores.

> 1 large cucumber, peeled, deseeded, and chopped
> 1 large red bell pepper, chopped
> 2 large ripe tomatoes, chopped
> 3–4 scallions, chopped
> 1 (15-ounce) can chickpeas, rinsed and drained
>   (or 1½ cups cooked chickpeas)
> 1 cup crumbled feta cheese
> ¼ cup minced fresh parsley
> ½ cup tangy black olives, pitted and halved
> 3–4 tablespoons extra virgin olive oil
> 2 tablespoons lemon juice
> ½ teaspoon zatar
> Salt and freshly ground black pepper, to taste
> Pita Crisps (page 225)

Place the cucumbers, bell pepper, tomatoes, scallions, chickpeas, cheese, parsley, and olives in a bowl and toss ingredients gently. Just before serving, mix together the olive oil, lemon juice, and zatar. Pour over the salad. Season to taste with salt and pepper. Serve with Pita Crisps. Makes 4 servings.

Minted Tomatoes

Few foods are quite as delicious as a fresh, ripe summer tomato. You can eat it out of hand, giving it a sprinkle of salt—or not! Tomatoes are also wonderful vehicles for certain vegetables and herbs: lettuce and basil are well known, but scallions and mint offer a sensational refreshing quality. This salad is especially good with grilled meats.

> 2 large tomatoes, chopped
> 4 chopped scallions
> ½ cup minced fresh mint
> 3 tablespoons extra virgin olive oil
> Salt, to taste

Place the tomatoes, scallions, mint, olive oil, and salt in a bowl. Toss, let rest for 5–10 minutes and serve. Makes 4 servings.

Quinoa Salad with Beans, Corn, and Peppers

It's easy to transform cooked grains into exciting salads. Mix in a few vegetables and a homemade vinaigrette, and you've got a good side dish. Make it into more of a substantial dinner salad by adding cooked chicken or turkey.

1 cup quinoa
1 (15-ounce) can black beans, rinsed and drained
1 cup cherry or grape tomatoes, cut in half
1 cup thawed frozen corn kernels
½ small red bell pepper, cut into ¼-inch pieces
3–4 scallions, chopped
1 small jalapeño pepper, deseeded and minced, optional
3 tablespoons minced fresh flat-leaf parsley
6 tablespoons extra virgin olive oil
3 tablespoons lime juice
2 tablespoons lemon juice
1 teaspoon ground cumin
Salt and freshly ground black pepper, to taste

Combine quinoa and 2 cups water in a medium saucepan, bring to a boil, reduce the heat and simmer, covered, for about 12–15 minutes or until the water is absorbed. Place the quinoa in a bowl and fluff with a fork. Add the beans, tomatoes, corn, bell pepper, scallions, jalapeño pepper, and parsley. Toss ingredients gently. In another bowl, combine the olive oil, lime juice, lemon juice, and cumin. Pour the dressing over the ingredients and toss gently. Season to taste with salt and pepper. Makes 4–6 servings.

Rice Salad with Raisins and Cashews

Using rice for salad opens up a world of possibilities. These days, we can buy several varieties and subvarieties of rice including white (basmati, jasmine, and so on) and several types of brown rice. White rice has the virtue of cooking faster, but if you prefer the more nutritious brown rice, you can use it here. Even though there's just a hint of cinnamon in this recipe, it's enough to enhance flavor ever so subtly. The salad would be equally good if you switched to chopped dates instead of raisins.

> 1 cup white rice
> 1 cup golden raisins
> 1 cut coarsely chopped cashews
> 4–6 scallions, chopped
> 3 tablespoons minced fresh parsley
> ¼ cup extra virgin olive oil
> 3 tablespoons lemon juice
> 2 tablespoons mayonnaise
> ¹⁄₁₆ teaspoon ground cinnamon
> Salt and freshly ground black pepper, to taste

Place the rice and 1¾ cups water in a medium saucepan and bring the liquid to a boil over high heat. Turn the heat to low, cover the pan, and cook for 18 minutes or until water has been absorbed. Remove the pan from the heat and let rest for 5 minutes. Spoon the rice into a mixing bowl. If you have time, wait at least 15 minutes to let the rice cool down. Add the raisins, cashews, scallions, and parsley and toss the ingredients to distribute them evenly. Mix the olive oil, lemon juice, and mayonnaise together and pour over the salad. Sprinkle in the cinnamon. Toss to coat the ingredients with the dressing. Season to taste with salt and pepper. Makes 6 servings.

Potato-Corn Salad with Basil Vinaigrette

Recipes for potato salad could fill an entire book. Cooked potatoes are mild enough to partner with many flavors, so you can dress the salad with mayonnaise or white wine or vinaigrette, add whatever vegetables you like, and season with salt and pepper only or with almost any herb or spice. This version includes corn kernels. You can use thawed, frozen kernels without cooking them (simply let them defrost) or leftover cooked kernels scraped from the cob with a large, sharp knife. If you have leftover grilled corn, even better—it will add a slightly smoky taste to the salad.

> 2 pounds small red bliss potatoes
> 1½ cups cooked or thawed frozen corn kernels
> ½ cup chopped sweet onion (such as Vidalia)
> 1 medium garlic clove, minced
> ¼ cup minced fresh basil
> 6 tablespoons extra virgin olive oil
> 3 tablespoons white wine vinegar
> 1 teaspoon Dijon mustard
> Salt and freshly ground black pepper, to taste

Cook the potatoes in lightly salted water for about 15 minutes or until they are fork tender. Drain the potatoes and peel them, if desired. Cut them into bite-size pieces and place in a bowl. Add the corn kernels, onion, garlic, and basil. Mix together the olive oil, vinegar, and mustard and pour over the potatoes. Season to taste with salt and pepper. Makes 6 servings.

You'll see several kinds of chile peppers in the store. Here's how they measure up on the heat scale:

Hot peppers include:
- ♨ Cayenne: finger-shaped, about 5 inches long, red or green
- ♨ Habanero: pointy-bottomed and bulbous, yellow, green, orange, or red
- ♨ Scotch bonnet: round-bottomed and bulbous, yellow, green, or red
- ♨ Pequin: small, tapered, red or green

(Continues on page 63)

Tomato-Avocado Salad

This versatile dish is like a chunky, simplified guacamole. It goes perfectly with the Cheese and Corn Arepas with Eggs (page 150) and also with grilled meats and poultry, but you can also spoon it on top of crackers for hors d'oeuvres. If you want to add some heat, mix in a small amount of chopped fresh jalapeño or, for even more intense heat, habanero pepper.

> 2 large, ripe tomatoes
> 2 small, ripe Hass avocados
> ¼ cup chopped red onion
> 2 tablespoons extra virgin olive oil
> 2 tablespoons lime juice
> 1–2 tablespoons minced fresh cilantro
> ⅛ teaspoon ground cumin
> Salt, to taste

Cut the tomato into bite-size pieces and place in a bowl. Peel the avocado and cut the flesh into bite-size pieces. Add the avocado and onion to the tomatoes. Pour in the olive oil and lime juice, add the cilantro, and sprinkle lightly with cumin and salt to taste. Toss ingredients gently. Makes 4 servings.

(Continued from page 62)

Medium hot peppers include:
- Chile de Arbol: slender, tapered, red or green
- Jalapeño: squat and conical, dark green or red
- Serrano: slim and cylindrical, green or red

Mildly hot peppers include:
- Poblano: large, triangular shape, red or dark green
- Anaheim: long and slender, rounded tapered end, green or red

To remove skin and pit from avocados, cut the avocado vertically with a sharp knife until you reach the pit. Cut all the way around the outside, hold both sides with two hands and twist to separate the halves. Stick the tip of a knife blade into the pit and twist until the pit releases. Scoop the flesh from the skin with a large spoon.

Grapefruit and Orange Salad with Mint Dressing

This is a refreshing salad that's perfect for a lazy weekend breakfast. It pairs nicely with fresh bagels, brioches, or muffins. Add a scoop of orange sorbet and it becomes dessert.

> 2 large pink or red grapefruit
> 4 large navel oranges
> 1 cup seedless red grapes, cut in half
> ¼ cup minced fresh mint
> 3 tablespoons honey
> 2 teaspoons fresh lime juice

Cut the grapefruits and oranges in half crosswise. Cut the flesh into segments and scoop them into a bowl. Add the grapes. Sprinkle in the mint and pour in the honey and lime juice. Toss the ingredients. Let rest about 10 minutes before serving. Makes 4–6 servings.

A grapefruit knife would be very handy for this dish—
the curve of the blade and the serrated edges make it
a cinch to scoop the fruit from skin and membranes.

GRAINS
AND PASTA

More and more people have turned to vegetarianism in recent years, some because of a moral or ethical conviction about killing and eating animals, others because of environmental issues or health concerns about animal fats and cholesterol. I'm not a vegetarian, although my menus include much less meat these days and our family often enjoys meatless dining.

There are a number of benefits to meat-free meals. For one thing, it's a good way to eat more of the type of lowfat, high-fiber diet recommended by doctors and nutritionists. Scientific studies have shown that eating a diet loaded with whole grains and other vegetarian staples can help lower the risk of heart disease, high blood pressure, diabetes, obesity, and some forms of cancer. I also don't like to eat the same food over and over and I think that branching out and incorporating grains, legumes, and other substantial nonmeat foods into our family meals is a good way to make those meals more varied and therefore more interesting.

Die-hard meat-and-potato fans sometimes fear that a vegetarian meal won't be hearty enough to be satisfying. And yet dishes made with whole grains and pastas are frequently filling, making it less likely that you will consume huge amounts of calories. A few good recipes transform familiar ingredients into Bulgur Wheat with Lentils, Caramelized Onions and Mushrooms (page 67), or Penne with Artichokes, Sun-Dried Tomatoes, and Olives (page 70), both flavorful and nourishing.

Some grains take a long time to cook but many don't. If you choose quinoa, bulgur wheat, or white rice, you can get dinner done in about a half hour; brown rice may need ten more minutes.

Kosher cooks often turn to grains and pasta because they are pareve and, while they are wonderful as part of a vegetarian meal, they can also be eaten with meat, fish, or dairy products. Raisin Curry Noodles (page 77) would be perfect in the same meal as a Spinach Pie (page 162); Tabbouleh (page 79) is wonderful with fish; Couscous with Dried Cranberries and Toasted Almonds (page 68) would be delicious with Pomegranate-Glazed Turkey London Broil (page 140).

Of course, although grains and pastas make wonderful vegetarian entrées and side dishes, you needn't limit them to meatless recipes. You can combine them in a dinner casserole with fish, meat, or poultry as in the colorful Stir-Fried Couscous with Chicken, Dried Apricots, and Pistachios (page 75).

Bulgur Wheat with Lentils, Caramelized Onions, and Mushrooms

This is a variation of a dish popular in the Middle East, where it is also prepared with brown or white rice. I've added mushrooms for a distinctly American touch. It's a recipe I also vary with frequency, adding tidbits of cooked broccoli, carrots, or peas and even pieces of leftover meat or poultry. Depending on the kind of meal I am serving I use chicken or beef stock instead of water. For a pareve accompaniment, try this with Minted Tomatoes (page 59); for a dairy meal, serve with Tzadziki (page 163).

> ¾ cup lentils
> 3 cups water or stock
> 1 cup fine-grain bulgur wheat
> 6–8 tablespoons extra virgin olive oil
> 2 large Vidalia onions (or 4–5 medium yellow onions),
>   sliced
> 10 ounces mushrooms, sliced
> ¼ cup minced fresh parsley
> Salt and freshly ground black pepper, to taste

Place the lentils and water or stock in a saucepan and bring to a boil over high heat. Turn the heat to low, cover the pan, and cook for 18–20 minutes. Add the bulgur wheat and stir gently. Cover the pan and cook for another 5 minutes or until the bulgur and lentils are tender and all the liquid has been absorbed. Remove the pan from the heat and let rest for 5 minutes. While the bulgur and lentils are cooking, heat 4 tablespoons olive oil in a sauté pan over medium-high heat. Add the onions and cook, stirring occasionally, for about 10 minutes or until beginning to brown. Add the mushrooms and cook for another 6–8 minutes or until the vegetables are golden brown. Add the parsley and stir. Transfer the bulgur and lentils to a bowl. Add about 2 tablespoons olive oil (a bit more if the grains seem dry) and mix. Season to taste with salt and pepper. Top with the sautéed onions and mushrooms and stir gently to incorporate some into the grain mixture. Makes 4 servings.

Couscous with Dried Cranberries
and Toasted Almonds

Tiny balls of Israeli couscous are the culinary pearls of the pasta world. Like any pasta, couscous can be covered with sauce or put it into soup, and it is first-rate for salad because it looks good and mixes well with other small salad items. This recipe combines sweet and piquant flavors in one dish. It's a treat with grilled meat or poultry, but also can be used as a snack or hors d'oeuvre.

1 cup Israeli couscous
¼ cup chopped or slivered almonds
⅓ cup dried cranberries
3–4 medium scallions, chopped
3 tablespoons extra virgin olive oil
1 tablespoon white wine vinegar
1 teaspoon finely grated fresh orange peel
Salt and freshly ground black pepper, to taste

Place the couscous in a dry sauté pan over medium heat and cook for 3–4 minutes, shaking the pan occasionally, until the couscous is lightly toasted. Place the couscous in a saucepan, add 1½ cups water and bring to a boil over high heat. Reduce the heat to low and cover the pan. Cook for 8–9 minutes or until all the water has been absorbed and spoon it into a bowl. While the couscous is cooking, toast the almonds in the sauté pan over medium heat for 4–5 minutes or until they are lightly browned. Add to the couscous. Stir in the cranberries and scallions and toss ingredients to distribute them evenly. Mix the olive oil, vinegar, and orange peel in a small bowl and pour over the couscous. Toss the ingredients and season to taste with salt and pepper. Makes 4–6 servings.

Curried Quinoa Stir-Fry

Quinoa is fairly new to the American market but this whole grain has been around for thousands of years. It is indigenous to the Andes mountains of South America and was one of the staple foods of the ancient Incas. The beads are small and crunchy and they have a nutty flavor. You can use quinoa like rice: serve it plain or as a salad, casserole, or pilaf. It has nutritious benefits, too. It is high in fiber and higher in protein than many other grains, containing nine essential amino acids.

> 1 cup quinoa
> ¼ cup extra virgin olive oil
> 1 medium onion, chopped
> ½ small red bell pepper, chopped
> ½ cup thawed frozen peas
> ¼ cup chopped dried apricots
> ¼ cup toasted cashews
> 1 teaspoon curry powder
> Salt and freshly ground black pepper, to taste
> 1 cup firm tofu, cut into small cubes
> 1 tablespoon minced fresh parsley

Bring 2 cups water to a boil in a saucepan over high heat and add the quinoa. Lower the heat, cover the pan, and simmer for 15–20 minutes or until all the water has been absorbed. Set aside. Heat the olive oil in a wok, stir-fry pan, or sauté pan over medium heat. Add the onion and bell pepper and cook for 2–3 minutes or until softened. Add the peas, apricots, cashews, curry powder, and salt and pepper to taste and cook for 1 minute. Add the quinoa and cook, stirring to distribute ingredients evenly. Add the tofu and toss the ingredients gently. Cook for 1–2 minutes or until the ingredients are hot. Dish out and sprinkle with parsley. Makes 4 servings.

Natural quinoa is covered with saponin, a natural substance that protects the seeds by repelling insects and birds. It is important to rinse the grains under cold water to remove it (it tastes bitter) but most packaged brands, available in traditional supermarkets as well as specialty stores, are already rinsed.

Penne with Artichokes, Sun-Dried Tomatoes, and Olives

This is the kind of dish that comes from making things up as you go along and also not wanting to waste food. One day when I was alone for dinner, I looked through the fridge and saw that I had a couple of artichoke hearts and some sun-dried tomatoes and olives. I decided to make things easy for myself, so I sautéed them together in a pan and added some pasta. It was so good—a lot depends on the type and quality of the olives—that I decided to make it again. This time I added some cheese and basil and everyone loved it. If you have marinated mushrooms or peppers, you can add those too. Or mix in small chunks of mozzarella cheese. You almost can't go wrong pairing leftover deli items and pasta.

> 1 pound penne pasta
> 6 large oil-packed artichoke hearts, coarsely chopped
> ½ cup oil-packed sun-dried tomatoes, coarsely chopped
> ½ cup pitted imported black, green, or mixed olives, coarsely chopped
> 2 large garlic cloves, minced
> ⅓ cup minced fresh basil
> 1 cup freshly grated Parmesan cheese
> Salt and freshly ground black pepper, to taste

Cook the pasta in lightly salted water until it is al dente. Drain, saving ¼ cup cooking water, and set aside. While the pasta is cooking, heat about 2 tablespoons of the oil from the artichokes or sun-dried tomatoes in a large sauté pan over medium heat. Add the artichokes, sun-dried tomatoes, olives, garlic, and basil and cook, stirring occasionally, for 2 minutes. Add the drained pasta, ½ cup of the cheese, and 3–4 tablespoons of the pasta cooking water. Season to taste with salt and pepper. Top with remaining cheese. Makes 4 servings.

In this and the following pasta dishes, prepare the ingredients (chopping the artichokes and sun-dried tomatoes, for example) before you cook the pasta. That way you can cook the sauce while the pasta is boiling and it will be ready when the pasta is ready.

Pasta with Raisins, Capers, and Pine Nuts

This dish will give you a taste of Sicily, where the strong, dominant flavors of ingredients such as capers, anchovies, raisins, and pine nuts prevail. The buttery, toasty-tasting bread crumbs give the dish an irresistibly crispy finish.

> ½ cup raisins
> 1 pound penne or other tubular pasta
> ½ cup extra virgin olive oil
> ⅓ cup plain dry bread crumbs
> 2 tablespoons butter
> 3 tablespoons pine nuts
> 3 tablespoons drained capers
> 6 anchovy fillets, mashed
> Salt and freshly ground black pepper, to taste

Place the raisins in a small bowl and cover them with warm water. Set aside. Cook the pasta in lightly salted water until it is al dente. Drain, saving ¼ cup cooking water, and set aside. While the pasta is cooking, heat 1 tablespoon olive oil in a small pan over medium heat. Add the bread crumbs and cook, stirring frequently, for 4 minutes or until they are golden brown. Set aside. Drain the raisins. Heat the butter plus 1 tablespoon olive oil in a large sauté pan over medium heat. When the butter has melted and looks foamy add the pine nuts and cook for 3–4 minutes or until lightly browned. Add the capers, raisins, and anchovy fillets. Cook, stirring frequently, for about 2 minutes. Add the drained pasta, the remaining 6 tablespoons olive oil, and cook, stirring to break up the pieces and coat them with the sauce. Pour in the pasta cooking water and season to taste with salt and pepper. Cook for another minute or so until the pasta is hot and completely glazed, then sprinkle in the bread crumbs. Toss a few times to coat the pasta with the crumbs. Makes 4 servings.

Stir-Fried Brown Rice
with Turkey and Mushrooms

This is the kind of dish you can throw together for an easy dinner, especially if you have leftover rice. You can vary the ingredients at will. I have used white basmati rice, corn, and lima beans instead of brown rice and peas and have used leftover turkey and chicken instead of raw. Sometimes I replace the curry with a tablespoon of fresh chopped herbs just to change the taste.

1 cup brown rice
1¾ cups plus 2 tablespoons water or stock
5 tablespoons vegetable oil
2 large eggs, beaten
4 thick scallions, chopped
2 garlic cloves, minced
10 ounces coarsely chopped mushrooms
½ pound diced raw turkey meat (½-inch pieces)
1 cup frozen peas
1 teaspoon curry powder
Salt and freshly ground black pepper, to taste

Place the rice and liquid in a saucepan. Bring to a boil over high heat and cook for 2 minutes. Lower the heat, cover the pan, and cook for 30 minutes or until the rice is tender but still slightly chewy (if all the liquid has not been absorbed drain the rice). Let cool. Heat 1 tablespoon oil in a wok, stir-fry pan, or sauté pan over medium heat. Add the eggs and cook them, stirring occasionally, until set. Dish out, chop the eggs coarsely and set them aside. Add 2 tablespoons oil to the pan. Add the scallions and cook for 1 minute. Add the garlic and mushrooms and cook for 2–3 minutes or until they have softened. Dish out and set aside. Add the remaining 2 tablespoons oil to the pan. Add the turkey and cook, stirring often, for 2–3 minutes or until all traces of pink have disappeared. Return the vegetables to the pan and add the rice, eggs, peas, and curry powder. Cook, stirring often for a minute or so or until the ingredients are hot and well mixed. Season to taste with salt and pepper. Makes 4 servings.

Fried rice should always be made using cool rice. Hot rice is too sticky.

Macaroni with Gorgonzola Cheese
and Bread Crumb–Walnut Crust

Everyone loves mac 'n' cheese! This is a more sophisticated version with tangy blue-veined cheese filling in for the standard cheddar. The nut and bread crumb crust makes a satisfyingly crunchy and vaguely sweet contrast to the soft, tangy pasta and sauce.

1½ cups elbow macaroni
4 tablespoons butter
2 tablespoons all-purpose flour
2 cups milk
½ teaspoon salt, or to taste
Freshly ground black pepper, to taste
1 cup crumbled blue-veined cheese
½ cup fresh bread crumbs
¼ cup finely chopped walnuts

Preheat the oven to 350°F. Cook the macaroni in lightly salted water until it is almost al dente. Drain and set aside in a bowl. While the macaroni is cooking, heat 2 tablespoons butter in a saucepan over medium heat. When the butter has melted and looks foamy turn the heat to low and add 2 tablespoons flour. Cook, stirring constantly with a whisk for 2–3 minutes. Gradually add the milk, stirring almost constantly for 3–4 minutes, or until a smooth sauce has formed. Stir in the salt, pepper, and cheese and continue to cook, stirring with the whisk or a wooden spoon for 3–4 minutes or until the cheese has melted and the sauce is smooth. Pour the sauce over the cooked macaroni and mix thoroughly. Place in a baking dish. Melt the remaining 2 tablespoons butter. Mix the bread crumbs, walnuts, and melted butter. Sprinkle over the macaroni. Bake for 10–15 minutes or until the crust is lightly browned and the cheese is melted and bubbly. Makes 4 servings.

In classic French cooking, the butter-flour mixture used here for macaroni and cheese is called a *roux*, which is the foundation for several sauces including béchamel or white sauce (milk is added to the *roux*) as well as Mornay (white sauce with cheese) and velouté (made with stock rather than milk).

Pasta with Eggplant, Tomatoes, and Mozzarella Cheese

When I have a craving for food that's old-fashioned but light and fresh, I make this for dinner. It's an all-season favorite, a pleasant dish that pairs nicely with a salad and a glass of red wine. It's best with fresh mozzarella cheese, but if you can't get that, packaged is just fine.

½ cup extra virgin olive oil
4–6 cups cut-up eggplant (¾-inch cubes)
1 medium onion, chopped
2 large garlic cloves, minced
8–10 large plum tomatoes, cut up
½ cup minced fresh basil
1 pound cooked ziti or penne
12 ounces mozzarella cheese, shredded
Salt and freshly ground black pepper, to taste
Freshly grated Parmesan cheese

Heat ¼ cup olive oil in a large nonstick sauté pan over medium heat. Add the eggplant and cook, stirring and tossing the cubes often, for about 6 minutes. Add the onion and cook for another 2–3 minutes. Add the garlic and cook briefly. Add 2 tablespoons olive oil to the pan. Add the tomatoes and basil and simmer for 5–6 minutes or until the tomatoes have softened. While the sauce is cooking, cook the pasta in lightly salted water until it is al dente. Drain, saving ¼ cup cooking water. Add the pasta to the sauce and mix. Add the remaining 2 tablespoons olive oil and the mozzarella cheese. Toss the ingredients and add some of the cooking water if needed for moisture. Season to taste with salt and pepper. Serve with the Parmesan cheese. Makes 4 servings.

Stir-Fried Couscous
with Chicken, Dried Apricots, and Pistachios

This is an easy pasta stir-fry that makes a quick dinner during the week. Because it's colorful and has a variety of textures, it also works well as a buffet item for a party. For a more substantial dinner, Carrot and Parsnip Soup (page 28) would make a fitting first course.

> 1¾ cups Israeli couscous
> 4 tablespoons extra virgin olive oil
> 20 ounces boneless chicken breast, cut into
>   bite-size chunks
> 4 thick scallions, chopped
> 1 cup chopped dried apricots
> 1 teaspoon ground cumin
> 1 teaspoon ground cinnamon
> 1 cup shelled pistachios
> Salt and freshly ground black pepper, to taste

Make the couscous according to the package directions. Set aside. Heat 2 tablespoons olive oil in a wok, stir-fry pan, or sauté pan over medium heat. Add the chicken and stir-fry for about 4 minutes or until the meat is white and cooked through. Dish out and set aside. Place the remaining 2 tablespoons olive oil in the pan. Add the scallions and cook for 1–2 minutes or until softened. Add the apricots, cumin, and cinnamon and cook, stirring constantly, for another minute. Add the couscous and chicken and stir-fry for 2–3 minutes to distribute the ingredients well. Stir in the pistachio nuts. Season to taste with salt and pepper. Eat hot or let cool to lukewarm. Makes 4 servings.

Pasta with Wild Mushrooms

This recipe is perfect when you're in a rush because all the ingredients cook so quickly. You can use common white mushrooms rather than wild mushrooms and for a more intense taste, when there's more time, you can add ¼ to ⅓ cup soaked and chopped dried mushrooms. If you include dried mushrooms soak them first in hot water for about 15–20 minutes to soften them.

> 1 pound small tubular pasta such as tubetti
> 4 tablespoons butter
> 4 tablespoons extra virgin olive oil
> 1 medium onion, chopped
> 1½ pounds assorted wild mushrooms, chopped coarsely
> 2 large garlic cloves, chopped
> ½ cup minced fresh parsley, preferably flat leaf
> Salt and freshly ground black pepper, to taste
> Pinch or two of cayenne pepper, optional
> ½ cup freshly grated Parmesan cheese

Cook the pasta in lightly salted water until it is al dente. Drain, saving ¼ cup of the cooking water, and set aside. While the pasta is cooking, heat the butter and 2 tablespoons olive oil in a large sauté pan over medium heat. When the butter has melted and looks foamy, add the onion and cook for 2–3 minutes or until slightly softened. Add the mushrooms and cook for 3–4 minutes. Add the garlic and parsley and continue cooking for 2–3 minutes or until most of the juices have evaporated and the mushrooms are golden brown. Season to taste with salt, pepper, and cayenne. Add the pasta to the mushroom mixture. Pour in the remaining 2 tablespoons olive oil and sprinkle in the cheese. Toss ingredients and add some of the pasta cooking water if needed for moisture. Makes 4 servings.

Pasta comes in a variety of shapes, all meant for different purposes. In general, small shapes such as tubetti are used for soup because they fit onto a spoon, but they are suggested here because the mushrooms shrink as they cook and would get lost within larger noodles, strings, or tubes. String pastas such as spaghetti are preferable for smooth sauces; large tubular pastas like ziti, penne, and rigatoni are best for chunky sauces.

Many so-called wild mushrooms are now cultivated but are generally labeled "wild" in markets. Some familiar varieties include cremini, oyster, portobello, shiitake, chanterelle, and hen-of-the-woods.

Raisin Curry Noodles

Kugel is an Eastern European Jewish favorite. It's a pudding usually made with noodles, eggs, and mild cheese (such as cottage cheese or cream cheese). This "nouvelle kugel" brings in a savory element by including curry powder and sharp, tangy cheddar. It is a lovely accompaniment to baked or grilled fish or as part of a dairy vegetarian meal. Some suitable partners include Bulgur Wheat with Lentils, Caramelized Onions, and Mushrooms (page 67), Couscous with Dried Cranberries and Toasted Almonds (page 68), Curried Quinoa Stir-Fry (page 69), Grilled or Broiled Salmon with Pineapple-Mango Salsa (page 83), and Roasted Pistachio-Crusted Salmon (page 98). Or serve it for brunch with muffins and fresh, cut-up fruit. You can make this a day or two ahead and store it in the fridge (rewarm at 350°F).

8 ounces wide egg noodles
1 cup dairy sour cream
1¼ cups cottage cheese
2 large eggs
1 teaspoon curry powder
½ teaspoon salt, or to taste
½ cup raisins
1 cup tightly packed, fresh bread crumbs
2 tablespoons melted butter
½ cup shredded cheddar cheese

Preheat the oven to 350°F. Cook the noodles in a large saucepan until they are al dente, drain, and return them to the pan. Add the dairy sour cream, cottage cheese, eggs, curry powder, salt, and raisins. Mix the ingredients thoroughly. Place the mixture in a baking dish. Combine the bread crumbs and butter and sprinkle on top of the noodles. Top with the cheddar cheese. Bake for 20 minutes or until the cheese has melted and the crust is lightly crispy. Makes 4 servings.

Rotelle with Smoked Salmon and Dill

This is a lavish dish, creamy and smoky tasting. It's an elegant choice for dinner, say, on a weekend night, especially good with a crisp white wine. If you're entertaining, consider serving the pasta topped a dollop of salmon caviar.

> 1 pound rotelle or other corkscrew-shaped pasta
> 2 tablespoons extra virgin olive oil
> 2 tablespoons butter
> 3–4 thick scallions, chopped
> 2 garlic cloves, minced
> 1 cup half-and-half cream
> 1 cup thawed frozen peas
> 2 teaspoons finely grated fresh lemon peel
> ¼ cup minced fresh dill
> 6 ounces sliced smoked salmon, cut crosswise into
>   thin strips
> ½ cup freshly grated Parmesan cheese
> Salt and freshly ground black pepper, to taste

Cook the rotelle in lightly salted water until it is al dente. Drain, saving ¼ cup of the cooking water, and set aside. While the pasta is cooking, heat the olive oil and butter in a large sauté pan over medium heat. When the butter has melted and looks foamy, add the scallions and cook for about 2 minutes or until softened slightly. Add the garlic and cream and cook for 3–4 minutes or until thickened slightly. Add the peas, lemon peel, and dill and heat to a simmer. Add the pasta and toss to coat it completely. Add the smoked salmon and Parmesan cheese and toss ingredients again. Add some of the pasta cooking water if needed for moisture. Season to taste with salt and pepper. Makes 4 servings.

Tabbouleh

This recipe was given to me by my friend Jean-Louis Gerin, Maître Cuisinier de France, who was voted "Best Chef, Northeast" by the James Beard Foundation. He and his wife, Linda, have operated the acclaimed Restaurant Jean-Louis in Greenwich, Connecticut, for many years. Jean-Louis made this dish for my husband, Ed, and me once when we were at his house. I found it so refreshing and loved it so much that I asked him for the recipe. It is especially tasty with Pan-Seared Tilapia with Lemon, Shallots, and Browned Butter (page 95), or Roasted Halibut Steaks with Herbs and Spices (page 93).

> 1 medium tomato
> ¼ cup lemon juice
> ¼ cup extra virgin olive oil
> ½ medium cucumber
> ¼ cup raisins
> 1 cup couscous
> ½ teaspoon hot pepper sauce
> ¾ teaspoon cumin seed
> ¼ cup minced fresh mint
> Salt, to taste

Cut the tomato in half and squeeze the seeds and natural juices into the bowl of a food processor. Add the lemon juice and olive oil and process until well combined. Pour the liquid into a measuring cup and add enough water to make 1¼ cups. Set aside. Dice the tomato into ¼-inch pieces and place in a bowl. Peel the cucumber, remove the seeds, dice it into ¼-inch pieces, and add to the tomato. Add the raisins, couscous, the 1¼ cups liquid, and the hot pepper sauce. Stir to distribute ingredients and let rest for one hour.

Crush the cumin seeds slightly and add to the couscous. Add the fresh mint and toss the ingredients. Taste for seasoning and add salt to taste. Makes 4 servings.

Most couscous recipes use boiling water to cook the pasta grains. Jean-Louis uses cold water and lets the grains absorb the liquid slowly over time for maximum flavor. If you have no time, substitute near-boiling water and proceed with the recipe when the grains have absorbed the liquid.

Whole Wheat Linguine
with Asparagus and Grape Tomatoes

I make this dish a lot because it's quick and easy and also very adaptable. Sometimes I use string beans or snap peas instead of asparagus, sometimes I add sautéed mushrooms, cooked broccoli rabe, or even small pieces of fresh mozzarella cheese. To make it into a meat meal, delete the cheese and include bits of crisped chicken sausage. I've suggested using fresh pasta rather than dried because I think dried whole wheat pasta can taste bitter. Besides, fresh pasta takes less than 5 minutes to cook.

1 pound whole wheat linguine (fresh pasta preferable)
¼ cup extra virgin olive oil
1 small onion, sliced
¾ pound asparagus, cut into 2-inch pieces
2 cups grape tomatoes
2 tablespoons minced fresh parsley
1 cup freshly grated Parmesan cheese
Salt and freshly ground black pepper, to taste

Cook the pasta in lightly salted water in accordance with manufacturer's directions. Drain, saving about ½ cup of the cooking water, and set aside. While the pasta is cooking, heat the olive oil in a large sauté pan over medium heat. Add the onion and asparagus and cook for 3 minutes. Add the tomatoes and parsley and cook for another 2 minutes. Add the drained pasta and ¼ cup of the pasta cooking water and toss the ingredients. Sprinkle with ½ cup of the Parmesan cheese. Add more of the pasta cooking water if needed for moisture. Season to taste with salt and pepper. Serve the remaining Parmesan cheese separately. Makes 4 servings.

FISH

Just a few decades ago, there wasn't much variety when it came to buying fish. But stop by a store today and you'll see a wealth of different kinds of fillets, steaks, and whole fish. Depending on where you shop, you may have a choice of several species of salmon, from dark orange-red sockeye to rich, meaty king and you may be able to buy farmed Atlantic salmon or wild Pacific. Depending on the season you'll have your pick of robust bluefish or mild grouper, meaty sea bass, or delicate flounder. The choices give you infinite possibilities for making dinner.

Fish sales have soared for several reasons. First are the health benefits. Fish is an excellent source of high-quality protein but it's lower in unwanted fats than meat or poultry. Oily varieties including salmon and tuna contain abundant amounts of omega-3 fatty acids, which are beneficial to heart health.

Second, each fish species has its own unique flavor and texture, so it's unlikely that dinner will ever be the same old same old.

For the modern, busy home cook, fish is a boon because it never takes a lot of time to cook. Whether you choose Pan-Seared Snapper with Hot

Tomato Relish (page 92) or Roasted Pistachio-Crusted Salmon (page 98), dinner will be memorably delicious—but easy.

Fish is a special blessing for the kosher home cook because it is pareve. You can prepare it with dairy products, as with Pan-Seared Tilapia with Lemon, Shallots, and Browned Butter (page 95) or as a first course preceding a meat entrée, say, Broiled Branzini with Tomato-Olive Relish (page 85) followed by Lamb Oreganata (page 111).

Kosher Quick Guide

FISH

✓ Fish must have fins and scales.

✓ The scales must be of a type that can be removed without destroying the animal's skin.

✓ nonkosher fish include shellfish (shrimp, lobster, scallops, crab, oysters, mussels, and clams), mollusks (octopus and squid), fish without scales (catfish and monkfish), and fish with improper scales (shark, eel, and some turbots). Swordfish and sturgeon are in a special category, considered kosher by some, nonkosher by others.

✓ Fish don't require soaking or salting and the blood is not forbidden.

✓ Fish do not require ritual slaughter.

✓ Fish is pareve.

✓ A useful list of kosher and nonkosher fish can be found at www.kashrut.com and www.kosherquest.org.

Grilled or Broiled Salmon with Pineapple-Mango Salsa

There's a lot to love about salmon. It's fatty but not gamy and it has a mild but distinctive flavor. Its lovely color shows up well on a dinner plate. It's also healthy because it's loaded with omega-3 fatty acids, which are beneficial to the heart. For home cooks there's another big bonus—it doesn't take much to enhance plain old salmon: flavor it with a marinade or a fragrant rub or serve it with a relish, compound butter, or salsa.

> 2 cups diced fresh pineapple
> 1 cup chopped mango
> ½ cup chopped red onion
> 2 tablespoons minced fresh mint
> 2 teaspoons minced fresh ginger
> ½–1 teaspoon minced fresh chile pepper such as serrano
> 2 tablespoons lime juice
> 1 tablespoon honey
> Salt, to taste
> 4 salmon fillets or steaks, about 6 ounces each,
>   1–1 ¼ inches thick
> Extra virgin olive oil
> Freshly ground black pepper, to taste

Place the pineapple, mango, red onion, mint, ginger, and chile pepper in a bowl and toss ingredients to distribute them evenly. Add the lime juice and honey and mix well. Sprinkle with salt. Let rest for at least 15 minutes. Preheat an outdoor grill or oven broiler with the rack about 6 inches from the heat source (or use a grill pan). Brush the fish all over with olive oil and sprinkle with salt and pepper. Place the fish flesh side down, cover the grill or pan, and cook for 3 minutes. Gently lift the fish with a rigid spatula, taking care not to break the flesh. Turn the fish over. Cook, covered, for an additional 5–9 minutes, depending on thickness of fish and degree of doneness desired. Serve with the salsa. Makes 4 servings.

You'll find several kinds of salmon in the market. Wild salmon is leaner, farmed and organic salmons are milder tasting. There are also several species: Atlantic salmon and several Pacific varieties including king (Chinook, Alaskan), coho, chum, and sockeye (which is dark red). For recipe purposes they are interchangeable. You can

(Continues on page 84)

(Continued from page 83)

buy salmon either as a fillet or a steak and both are fine for broiling. Fillets are easier to handle because you don't have to bother with bones, which can be annoying, but many people prefer the steaks because the bones provide additional flavor. To be sure the fish browns nicely without overcooking, try to buy pieces that are at least 1 inch thick, and preferably 1¼ inches thick.

Baked Cod with Curry and Yogurt

This dish has the elements of Indian-style tandoori: food marinated in yogurt and curry seasonings cooked at high temperatures. Most of us don't have a tandoor (a special clay oven) but the dish is fragrant and flavorful anyway and crisps at the outer edge like any tandoori dish. If you have the time to marinate the fish for several hours in the seasoned yogurt, all the better. The more time you give it, the more intense the taste will be. Substitute fish include halibut, scrod, haddock, or grouper.

4 cod fillets, about 6–8 ounces each
½ cup plain yogurt
2 tablespoons lemon juice
1 large garlic clove, minced
1 teaspoon minced fresh ginger
½ teaspoon ground coriander
½ teaspoon ground turmeric
½ teaspoon ground cumin
¼ teaspoon paprika
⅛ teaspoon cayenne pepper
Pinch of ground cinnamon
Salt, to taste
Lime wedges

Preheat the oven to 450°F. Place the fish in a baking pan. Combine the yogurt, lemon juice, garlic, ginger, coriander, turmeric, cumin, paprika, cayenne, and cinnamon. Spoon the sauce over the fish and turn the fish to coat all sides. Sprinkle with salt. Let rest for 30 minutes or longer if possible. Bake for 12–15 minutes or until cooked through. Serve with lime wedges. Makes 4 servings.

Broiled Branzini with Tomato-Olive Relish

Branzini, also known as loup de mer, is mild and moist. You don't have to do much to it to make it tasty, just brush it with olive oil and season with salt and pepper and stick it under the broiler or on top of the grill for a few minutes. But plain broiled fish like this invites a good sauce, giving you an opportunity to serve a relish, salsa, or other sauce to serve as an accompaniment. This dish goes nicely with Zucchini Fritters (page 200).

> ¾ cup mixed, pitted Mediterranean olives
> 2 large tomatoes, chopped
> 2 large garlic cloves, minced
> 2 tablespoons minced fresh basil
> 2 tablespoons minced fresh parsley, preferably flat-leaf
> 2 tablespoons plus 2 teaspoons extra virgin olive oil
> 1–2 teaspoons lemon juice
> 4 branzini fillets, about 6–8 ounces each
> Salt and freshly ground black pepper, to taste

Preheat the oven broiler with the rack about 4 inches from the heat. In a bowl, combine the olives, tomatoes, garlic, basil, parsley, 1 tablespoon plus 2 teaspoons olive oil, and the lemon juice. Mix and set aside. Brush the fish with the remaining 1 tablespoon olive oil. Season to taste with salt and pepper. Broil the fish for 4–5 minutes, or until cooked through. Spoon the relish on each of four plates and top with the fish. Makes 4 servings.

Broiling fish can be tricky. If it's a thin fillet, like branzini, keep it close to the heat source (3–4 inches) so that the surface can crisp nicely in the short time it takes for the insides to cook. If the fish is thicker, move the heat source farther away so the outside won't char before the interior has cooked.

Mackerel Fillets
with Lime-Mustard Butter and Scallions

Every summer, when I was a kid, my dad and uncle would go on a once-a-year fishing trip. They'd take my brothers and some of their friends. Because we were girls, my cousin Leslie and I were never included, so on those days we went fishing on our own. We used skinny twigs for fishing rods, some of our mothers' yarn for string, and safety pins as hooks. We did catch a few minnows for our trouble, but threw them back. The men caught mackerel, which my grandma always broiled with lots of lemon or lime and mustard. I can still taste how delicious those days were.

4 tablespoons butter, softened

1 tablespoon Dijon mustard

2 tablespoon lime juice

1 teaspoon finely grated fresh lime peel

2 tablespoons minced fresh parsley

Salt and freshly ground black pepper, to taste

1 thick scallion, minced

4 mackerel fillets, about 6 ounces each

Preheat the oven broiler with the rack about 4 inches from the heat source. Mix the butter, mustard, lime juice, lime peel, parsley, pepper, and scallion together. Place the fish in a heatproof pan, skin side down. Brush with the lime butter. Broil for about 6 minutes, basting once or twice, or until cooked through. Makes 4 servings.

Baked Grouper with Tomatoes and Herbs

Sometimes you're in the mood for uncomplicated, familiar flavors like the ones in this dish. The mild herbs appeal even to children. Substitute fish include snapper, cod, Chilean sea bass, or halibut. Zucchini Fritters (page 200) and Mustard-Roasted Potatoes with Lemon-Oregano Dressing (page 189) are suitable side dishes.

> 4 grouper fillets
> 1 tablespoon extra virgin olive oil
> 2 tablespoons lemon juice
> Salt and freshly ground black pepper, to taste
> 1 shallot, chopped
> 2 large garlic cloves, minced
> 2 tomatoes, chopped
> 3 tablespoons minced fresh parsley
> 1 tablespoon minced fresh oregano
>   (or 1 teaspoon dried oregano)
> 1 tablespoon minced fresh basil
> ½ cup fresh bread crumbs

Preheat the oven to 450°F. Place the fillets in a baking dish and brush with 1 tablespoon olive oil. Sprinkle with the lemon juice. Season to taste with salt and pepper. Sprinkle the shallot, garlic, tomatoes, parsley, oregano, basil, and bread crumbs on top of the fish. Bake for 12–15 minutes or until the fish is cooked through and the bread crumbs are lightly browned. Makes 4 servings.

You can substitute a smaller amount of dried herbs in recipes but fresh herbs are widely available and offer a more vibrant taste to quickly cooked dishes like this one. They are also incredibly easy to grow, even indoors in an apartment, so if you cook with herbs with any frequency, think about an herb garden for your abode. It'll be convenient and save you money, too. Although there is no hard-and-fast rule, substituting dried herbs for fresh is about 3 to 1.

Baked Snapper *en Papillote*

Cooking *en papillote* is not only fast but beautiful. It involves wrapping the fish in a package that looks like a butterfly. The fish steams quickly inside the package so this method is perfect for all thin fillets. In addition to using snapper, you can try pompano, grouper, perch, or one of the flatfish (sole or flounder).

> 4 red snapper fillets with skin, about 6–8 ounces each,
> about 1 inch thick
> 1 tablespoon lemon juice
> Salt and freshly ground black pepper, to taste
> 2 tablespoons extra virgin olive oil
> 1 large shallot, chopped
> 1 cup cherry or grape tomatoes, cut in half
> ¼ cup chopped imported black olives
> 1½ tablespoons capers, drained and rinsed
> 2 tablespoons minced fresh basil
> ½ teaspoon red pepper flakes, optional

Preheat the oven to 425°F. Place each piece of fish on a piece of aluminum foil large enough to enclose the fish. Sprinkle with the lemon juice and salt and pepper to taste. Mix the olive oil, shallot, tomatoes, olives, capers, basil, and red pepper flakes and place equal quantities of the mixture on top of each fillet. Tightly wrap the fish by sealing the edges of the foil. Place the foil packages on a cookie sheet. Bake for 15 minutes. Serve in the package and let each person pierce the top and open the foil. Makes 4 servings.

Restaurants use parchment paper and serve the fish enclosed in the *papillote*. The paper puffs up with steam as it cooks and diners puncture the paper with the tip of a sharp knife. It's a lovely presentation for company. If you don't have parchment on hand, aluminum foil does the cooking job just as well.

Grilled or Broiled Salmon
with Ginger-Scallion-Cilantro Butter

Salmon is one of the most accommodating fish. You can poach, bake, sauté, or roast it and it doesn't fall apart easily. But grilling or broiling are among the easiest methods. My mother broiled salmon with a coating of milk because she said it kept the fish moist. I've tried the milk bath many times, but prefer the tried-and-true standby: I brush the fish with olive oil, sprinkle it with salt and pepper, and grill it about 6 inches from the heat for 8–10 minutes depending on how thick it is.

> 4 salmon fillets or steaks, about 6 ounces each,
>   about 1 to 1¼ inches thick
> 2 tablespoons teriyaki marinade
> 2 teaspoons honey Dijon mustard
> 3 tablespoons butter, at room temperature
> 1 teaspoon minced ginger
> 1 medium scallion, minced
> 1 teaspoon minced fresh cilantro
> 1½ teaspoons lemon juice or rice wine vinegar

Preheat an outdoor grill or oven broiler with the rack about 6 inches from the heat source (or use a grill pan). Mix the teriyaki marinade and mustard. Brush the salmon with the teriyaki mixture. Let rest for 15 minutes. Grill or broil the fish for about 8–10 minutes, depending on the thickness, or until cooked to the degree of doneness desired. While the fish is cooking, mix the butter, ginger, scallion, cilantro, and lemon juice in a small bowl. Serve each piece of salmon topped with some of the seasoned butter. Makes 4 servings.

You can cook salmon without turning it, but if you use an outdoor grill (or grill pan) and want those lovely-looking grid marks on the surface, place the fish flesh-side down, cover the grill or pan, and cook for 3 minutes. Gently lift the fish with a rigid spatula, taking care not to break the flesh. Turn the fish over. Cook, covered, for an additional 5–9 minutes, depending on thickness of fish and degree of doneness desired. Before cooking, be sure the grill or pan grids are well oiled, to prevent sticking.

Curry-Roasted Halibut with Curry-Coconut Butter

Roasting is a good method for cooking thick fish fillets and steaks. In a hot, pre-heated oven it should take only about 10 minutes for each inch of thickness. Sauce or a compound butter like the one in this recipe keeps the meaty flesh of a thick piece of fish deliciously moist. Substitute fish include cod, snapper, and grouper.

4 halibut fillets, about 6 ounces each,
    about 1¼ to 1½ inches thick
1 tablespoon vegetable oil
2 teaspoons cumin
Pinch of ground cinnamon
Pinch of cayenne pepper
Salt, to taste
3 tablespoons butter, softened
2 tablespoons minced coconut (packaged is fine)
1 teaspoon curry powder
Pinch ground cloves

Preheat the oven to 450°F. Place the fish in a baking dish, leaving room between each piece. Brush the top of each fillet with some of the vegetable oil. Sprinkle with the cumin, cinnamon, cayenne, and salt to taste. Roast for 12–15 minutes, depending on thickness, or until the fish is cooked through. While the fish is roasting, mix the butter, coconut, curry powder, and cloves until well blended. Place equal amounts of the butter on top of each portion of fish. Return the fish to the oven for about a half-minute or until the butter starts to melt. Makes 4 servings.

Packaged coconut is usually sweetened, but it won't detract from the recipe. Many curries include a sweetener of some sort to boost flavor. If you prefer, you can rinse the coconut or use unsweetened coconut.

Mustard-Panko-Crusted Sole

Sole is the perfect choice when you want a quick dinner. The fillets are thin and cook within minutes. Other flatfish like flounder and fluke will work with this recipe and you could also substitute thicker fish like grouper, haddock, or halibut fillets (adjust cooking times). Try this with Easy Beans (page 186) when you need a truly quick dinner. If you have more time consider Beet Greens with Red Onions and Raisins (page 188) or Eggplant with Yogurt and Pine Nuts (page 185).

> 3 tablespoons extra virgin olive oil
> 1 tablespoon Dijon mustard
> 2 tablespoons lemon juice
> 4 thin white-fleshed fish fillets (such as sole)
> 1½ cups panko
> 1½ teaspoons finely grated fresh lemon peel
> 1 teaspoon paprika
> ¾ teaspoon mustard seeds
> Salt, to taste

Preheat oven to 450°F. Mix the olive oil, mustard, and lemon juice and dredge the fillets in this mixture to coat them completely. Mix the panko with the lemon peel, paprika, mustard seeds, and salt to taste. Mix well to blend ingredients. Dredge the fillets in the panko and press onto the fish to coat all sides. Place the fish on a lightly oiled baking sheet. Bake for about 8 minutes, or until fish is cooked through and crust is lightly crispy. Makes 4 servings.

You can broil the fish if you prefer: set the rack about 4 inches from the heat source, turn once after 2 minutes, and cook for 5–6 minutes or until lightly browned and cooked through.

Pan-Seared Snapper with Hot Tomato Relish

Pan searing gives fish a crisp, golden crust. It helps to use a nonstick pan because the fish will brown well but not stick to the bottom. After the initial searing the fish goes into the oven for a few minutes so the insides can cook completely. Fish cooked this way are crispy outside, but stay lushly moist within. This dish would be nice with sautéed spinach or beet greens and Garlic and Scallion Smashed Potatoes (page 182).

2 cups halved grape tomatoes

2 tablespoons minced fresh parsley

2 teaspoons minced fresh thyme

2 thick scallions, chopped

Salt and freshly ground black pepper, to taste

4 tablespoons extra virgin olive oil

4 fillets of snapper, hake, sea bass, or other firm fish with
skin, about 1 inch thick

¼ cup all-purpose flour

2 tablespoons butter

Preheat the oven to 425°F. Combine the tomatoes, parsley, thyme, scallions, and salt and pepper to taste in a bowl. Pour in 2 tablespoons olive oil, mix, and set aside. Dredge the fish in flour and shake off the excess. Sprinkle with salt and pepper to taste. Heat the remaining 2 tablespoons olive oil with the butter in a large ovenproof sauté pan, preferably nonstick, over medium-high heat. When the butter has melted and looks foamy, add the fish, skin side down, and cook for about 3 minutes, or until the bottom is richly brown, pressing the top occasionally to keep the fish flat. Place the pan in the oven and cook for another 5 minutes or until cooked through. Place the fish on individual dishes. Spoon the tomato mixture into the sauté pan and cook for about 1 minute on high heat, stirring often, or until the tomatoes are hot. Spoon equal amounts of the hot tomato relish next to each serving of fish. Makes 4 servings.

Use red and yellow tomatoes for more vivid color.

Roasted Halibut Steaks with Herbs and Spices

Halibut is a firm white fish and has lots of flavor that stands up well to bold seasonings. You can mix the herb and spice mixture in this recipe in a matter of minutes, making this recipe a blessing on a truly busy day. Substitute fish include cod, haddock, grouper, and perch. Serve this with Stir-Fried Fennel (page 198) or Crisped Cauliflower with Raisins and Pine Nuts (page 181).

> 3 tablespoons extra virgin olive oil or softened butter
> 1 large garlic clove, minced
> 2 tablespoons minced fresh parsley
> 1 tablespoons minced fresh basil
> 1 tablespoon sweet paprika
> ½ teaspoon dried oregano
> ½ teaspoon salt
> ¼ teaspoon cayenne pepper
> 1 tablespoon fresh lemon juice
> 1 teaspoon finely grated fresh lemon peel
> 4 halibut steaks, about 1 inch thick
> Lemon wedges

Preheat the oven to 450°F. Mix the olive oil or butter with the garlic, parsley, basil, paprika, oregano, salt, cayenne, lemon juice, and lemon peel until well blended. Spread the mixture on both sides of the fish. Place fish in an ovenproof dish and roast for about 10 minutes, or until fish is cooked through. Serve with lemon wedges. Makes 4 servings.

Pepper-Crusted Bluefish
with Horseradish Yogurt Sauce

People seem to either love or hate bluefish. It has a rich, oily, dark flesh that some consider too "fishy." I disagree. Bluefish is one of my favorites because it is meaty and flavorful—the opposite of bland. It's also easy to cook. Grill or broil it plain and serve it with a bold sauce like the one in this recipe. Minted Tomatoes (page 59) or Sautéed Carrots with Mint and Shallots (page 194) are terrific accompaniments.

> 4 bluefish fillets, about 6–8 ounces each
> 1½ tablespoons extra virgin olive oil
> 2 teaspoons coarsely crushed black peppercorns
> Salt, to taste
> ½ cup mayonnaise
> ½ cup plain yogurt
> 2 tablespoons prepared white horseradish
> 1 tablespoon Dijon mustard
> 2 medium scallions, chopped
> 1 tablespoon drained capers, chopped
> 1 tablespoon fresh lemon juice

Preheat the oven broiler with the rack about 6 inches from the heat source. Place the fish in a broiling pan and brush with the olive oil. Sprinkle with the pepper and salt to taste. Broil for about 6–10 minutes, depending on thickness, or until cooked through. While the fish is cooking, prepare the sauce. Combine the mayonnaise, yogurt, horseradish, mustard, scallions, capers, and lemon juice in a bowl. Blend ingredients well. Serve the fish and sauce separately. Makes 4 servings.

The sauce is versatile enough for people who prefer to cut down on fat—make it with nonfat yogurt and lowfat mayonnaise. But for those who crave a rich accompaniment to fish—use dairy sour cream instead of yogurt. The recipe makes about one cup of sauce, which can also be used for other plain, broiled fish.

Pan-Seared Tilapia
with Lemon, Shallots, and Browned Butter

Most pan-seared fish are finished in a hot oven after the initial browning but to avoid overcooking in the case of tilapia and other thin fillets, the pan should be placed in a warm oven or on a serving platter and covered with aluminum foil (or, if you're lucky enough to have one, in a warming drawer).

>   4 tilapia fillets (or use porgy or sole)
>   Salt and freshly ground black pepper, to taste
>   ¼ cup all-purpose flour
>   4 tablespoons extra virgin olive oil
>   2 tablespoons butter
>   2 large shallots, chopped, about ⅓ cup
>   3 tablespoons minced fresh chives
>   3 tablespoons minced fresh parsley
>   8 thin lemon slices
>   ½ cup dry white wine, or fish or vegetable stock

Preheat the oven to warm, 140°F. Sprinkle the fish with salt and pepper to taste, then dredge in the flour. Shake off the excess flour. Heat 2 tablespoons olive oil and 2 tablespoons butter in a large sauté pan, preferably nonstick, over medium-high heat. When butter has melted and looks foamy, add the fish. Cook for about 4 minutes, or until nicely browned. Turn the fish and cook for an additional 2–3 minutes. Transfer the fish to a serving platter and keep warm in the oven. Heat the 2 tablespoons remaining olive oil in the pan. Add the shallots and cook for 1 minute. Add the chives and parsley, and stir. Add the lemon slices, pour in the liquid, and cook for another minute or so, until the sauce has thickened slightly. Remove the pan from the heat. Transfer the fish to four plates. Top each fish with two of the lemon slices and spoon the pan contents over the fish. Makes 4 servings.

Roasted Haddock
with Tangerine-Paprika Panko Crust

This recipe is a little hot, a little sweet. The fruit and cinnamon complement the cayenne beautifully. If you can't find tangerines, Valencia (juice) oranges will be fine, just a bit sweeter. Blood oranges are a nice substitute also, if you can find them. Substitute fish include halibut, grouper, snapper, perch, and sea bass.

¼ cup fresh tangerine juice
2 tablespoons extra virgin olive oil
1 tablespoon fresh thyme leaves
1½ to 2 pounds haddock fillets
6 tablespoons panko bread crumbs
1 tablespoon paprika
⅛ teaspoon cayenne pepper
1 tablespoon brown sugar
½ teaspoon ground cinnamon
2 teaspoons grated tangerine peel
Salt, to taste

Combine the tangerine juice, olive oil, and thyme. Place the fish in a baking dish and pour the mixture on top. Turn the fish to coat both sides. Let rest for at least 15 minutes. Preheat the oven to 450°F. Mix the panko crumbs, paprika, cayenne, sugar, cinnamon, tangerine peel, and salt to taste. Coat the fish with the panko mixture. Roast for about 12–15 minutes or until cooked through. Makes 4 servings.

> The topping for the fish should be crisp. To prevent sogginess, use a pan that's large enough to hold the fish fillets comfortably without touching each other.

Sesame-Seared Tuna Steaks
with Cucumber and Tomato Salad

Tuna is meaty and looks a lot like beef, especially when cooked rare. The sesame seeds give the fish a nice crunchy crust that complements the softer salad ingredients.

¼ cup soy sauce
¼ cup mirin
2 teaspoons sesame oil
1 teaspoon brown sugar
4 tuna steaks, about 1½ inches thick, 6–8 ounces each
½ cup sesame seeds
3 tablespoons vegetable oil

Cucumber and Tomato Salad

1 cucumber, peeled, deseeded and cut into ¾-inch dice
1 cup grape tomatoes, cut into quarters
2 scallions, chopped
2 tablespoons vegetable oil
4 teaspoons rice vinegar
½ teaspoon minced fresh ginger
¼ teaspoon wasabi powder

Combine the soy sauce, mirin, sesame oil, and sugar in a bowl. Place the tuna in a shallow dish. Pour the dressing over the fish and let rest for 15–20 minutes. Place the sesame seeds on a dish and press the fish on the seeds to coat the surface. Heat the 3 tablespoons vegetable oil in a sauté pan over medium heat. Cook the fish for 3–4 minutes per side or until it reaches the degree of doneness desired. While the fish is cooking, combine the cucumber, tomatoes, and scallions and toss to distribute ingredients. Mix the 2 tablespoons vegetable oil, vinegar, ginger, and wasabi powder. Pour over the vegetables. Place the tuna on each of four plates accompanied by the salad. Makes 4 servings.

Roasted Pistachio-Crusted Salmon

Mustard and pistachios bring out the best in salmon. This recipe is so easy and the fish so flavorful that it's probably the one I make most often. I usually serve this dish with Stir-Fried Fennel (page 198), which adds a little style and flavor contrast, but it is also wonderful with Roasted Plum Tomatoes (page 191), Green Beans with Lime Butter (page 183), or Spinach with Garlic, Chile Pepper, and Lemon (page 196), or plain steamed brown rice and green salad.

    4 salmon fillets or steaks, about 6 ounces each, about
        1¼ inches thick
    1 tablespoon extra virgin olive oil
    2 tablespoons Dijon mustard
    2 teaspoons finely grated fresh lemon peel
    Freshly ground black pepper, to taste
    2 tablespoons crushed pistachios

Preheat the oven to 475°F. Place the salmon in a baking dish. Mix the olive oil, mustard, and lemon peel and spread this mixture evenly over the surface of the fish. Sprinkle with pepper and scatter the nuts evenly on top. Roast for about 12–15 minutes, depending on thickness, or until nearly cooked through but still darker in the thickest part of the center. Makes 4 servings.

> Keep some crushed nuts (pistachios, almonds, and so on) in small, airtight plastic bags in the freezer so that you don't have to process them every time you need them for a recipe.

Thai-Style Fish Curry

This dish has a thick, savory sauce that's hot but also faintly sweet, making it perfect with plain, steamed rice. You can cut down on the chile paste if you prefer a milder version. Substitute fish include haddock, snapper, and cod.

2 tablespoons vegetable oil
1 small onion, chopped
2 tablespoons chopped lemongrass or the grated peel of
    1 medium lemon
1 tablespoon minced fresh ginger
2 garlic cloves, minced
2 tablespoons chile paste (sambal)
1 teaspoon Worcestershire sauce
2 teaspoons ground cumin
½ teaspoon ground turmeric
1½ cups coconut milk
¾ cup fish or vegetable stock
Salt, to taste
1½–2 pounds sea bass fillets, about 1½ inches thick
2 tablespoons minced fresh cilantro

Heat the vegetable oil in a sauté pan over medium heat. Add the onion, lemongrass, ginger, and garlic and cook for 1–2 minutes or until softened. Add the chile paste, Worcestershire sauce, cumin, and turmeric and blend them into the vegetables. Pour in the coconut milk, stock, and salt. Stir and bring to a simmer. Add the fish, cover the pan, and simmer for 8–10 minutes or until cooked through. Transfer the fish to a platter. Raise the heat and boil the pan fluids for about 5 minutes or until thick enough to coat the back of a spoon. Return the fish to the pan (discard juices that may have accumulated in the plate) and heat through. Serve sprinkled with cilantro. Makes 4 servings.

If you use chile paste with garlic, omit the garlic in the recipe.

(Continued on next page)

Thai dishes frequently call for fish sauce, but, after searching high and low, I could not find a brand with a hekhsher. Regular Worcestershire sauce is the closest in taste and concept to fish sauce.

Lemongrass is an herb popular in Asian cooking. It tastes lightly lemony but is more pungent and aromatic than a standard citrus lemon. The stalks are sold fresh in produce sections of the supermarket. Peel away the hard, fibrous outer leaves and use only the tender bulb at the bottom. You needn't throw away the leaves. Use them to flavor a sweet poaching fluid for plums (see the recipe for Clove and Lemongrass–Poached Plums, page 221), peaches, pears, and other fruit or stuff them into the cavity of chickens or Cornish hens before roasting.

MEAT

Kosher meat presents some challenges for the home cook. As I mentioned in the section "What Does Kosher Mean?" with rare exceptions the only permissible cuts are those from the forequarter of the animal. Except for the meat in the rib section, and—if it's cooked right—the flavorful skirt steak (cut from the diaphragm), most kosher cuts are tough and require long, slow simmering. Kosher cuisine is abundant with fabulous braised beef briskets and short ribs, comforting beef and veal stews, and savory lamb shanks. Unfortunately, delicious though they are, those kinds of dishes require too much time for weekday meals. We have to look to grilling, broiling, and pan-frying to get a meat entrée done quickly.

Grilled rib steak is always a good bet. It's hard to get wrong and takes no time at all to cook, but Grilled Rib Steak with Spice Rub (page 106), jazzed up with a well-seasoned coating, is more interesting. Marinades also boost meat flavor, so that even when you cook shoulder Lamb Chops with Charmoula Pesto (page 107) or Skirt Steak with Orange-Chile Marinade and Fruit Salsa (page 114), you won't notice that the meat is a cut that isn't particularly tender.

Because kosher meat is soaked and salted, it can be very salty. Skirt steak is particularly problematic; this cut is koshered after its outer membrane has been removed, making it easier for the salt to infuse the meat. If you have time, soak skirt steak in cold water for about 30 minutes before you cook it. It's probably smart not to add salt to kosher meat recipes. My suggestion is to taste the food and add seasonings only as needed.

Butchers may label kosher cuts differently from place to place, but generally, the kosher beef cuts that do well when quickly cooked include rib, "filet split," Delmonico, shell, skirt, club, and hanger. For veal and lamb, look for rib or shoulder.

Kosher Quick Guide

MEAT

- ✓ Meat must come from an animal that has split hooves and chews its cud.
- ✓ Kosher meats include beef, buffalo, veal, lamb, mutton, goat, and venison.
- ✓ Pork, rabbit, horse, and the flesh of carnivorous animals are not kosher.
- ✓ Ritual slaughter must be performed by a professional (shochet).
- ✓ Kosher meat of cattle, sheep, and goats are most often limited to cuts from the forequarter of the animal.
- ✓ Kosher meat is soaked and salted to eliminate prohibited blood.

Beef Kebabs with Quick Pebre Sauce

Pebre sauce, a Chilean specialty, is a spicy, hot condiment for grilled beef or chicken. It's similar to chimichurri sauce, which has become popular in American cooking. Chimichurri sauce is available in jars, pebre sauce is not, which is actually a good thing, since nothing beats homemade, freshly concocted condiments like this one. You can use pebre as a dipping condiment for grilled skirt steak or hanger steak but because it also tastes so good on grilled vegetables, especially tomatoes, onions, and peppers, the sauce is especially handy for kebabs.

1 cup packed fresh flat-leaf parsley leaves

¼ cup fresh cilantro leaves

2 large garlic cloves, quartered

1 tablespoon fresh oregano leaves

2 tablespoons lemon juice

1 small habanero pepper, deseeded and quartered
    (or 1–1½ teaspoons hot pepper sauce)

½ cup extra virgin olive oil, plus more for brushing
    ingredients

2 pounds boneless beef for grilling

Large cherry tomatoes or other small whole tomatoes

1 large red or yellow bell pepper, deseeded, cut into
    chunks

2 medium onions, cut into 8 pieces

Preheat an outdoor grill or oven broiler with the rack about 4–6 inches from the heat source. To make the pebre sauce, place the parsley, cilantro, garlic, oregano, lemon juice, and habanero pepper in a food processor and process until the ingredients are finely minced. Gradually add ½ cup olive oil while the machine is on, until the sauce is thoroughly blended and the oil has been incorporated. Set aside. Cut the meat into 1- to 1½-inch chunks. Place alternating chunks of beef, tomatoes, bell pepper chunks, and onion pieces onto metal skewers. Brush the ingredients with a small amount of olive oil. Cook for about 7–12 minutes, turning the skewers occasionally, or until the meat reaches the degree of doneness desired. Serve with the pebre sauce. Makes 4 servings.

Boneless Lamb with Cumin and Ginger

This is a good dish to prep in the morning for dinner that evening. The marinade takes a few minutes to put together and isn't acidic, so the lamb can stay in it for up to 24 hours. The longer the meat marinates, the more intense the flavor. Good side dishes include Sautéed Carrots with Mint and Shallots (page 194), Easy Beans (page 186), and Garlic and Scallion Smashed Potatoes (page 182).

1½ teaspoons ground cumin
½ teaspoon red pepper flakes
½ teaspoon ground coriander
3 garlic cloves, minced
1 tablespoon minced fresh ginger
1½ teaspoons finely grated fresh lemon peel
2 tablespoons extra virgin olive oil
1½–2 pounds boneless lamb
Freshly ground black pepper, to taste

Preheat the oven broiler or outdoor grill with the rack about 4–6 inches from the heat source. Combine the cumin, red pepper flakes, coriander, garlic, ginger, lemon peel, and olive oil in a small bowl. Brush the seasoning over the meat and marinate for an hour or more if possible. Broil or grill for 4–8 minutes per side depending on thickness of the meat or until it has reached the degree of desired doneness. Season to taste with pepper. Makes 4 servings.

Grilled Hoisin-Scented Lamb Chops

Lamb has a distinctive taste that works well with bold flavorings and also sweet mellow ones such as the hoisin sauce and honey glaze in this recipe. You can also use this glaze for rib chops, rack of lamb, and kebabs.

2 tablespoons hoisin sauce
2 tablespoons honey
1 tablespoon soy sauce
1 tablespoon lemon juice
1 tablespoon vegetable oil
1 garlic clove, minced
1½ teaspoons minced fresh ginger
2 thick scallions, chopped
4 large shoulder lamb chops, about 1 inch thick

Preheat the oven broiler or outdoor grill with the rack about 4–6 inches from the heat source (or use a grill pan). Combine the hoisin sauce, honey, soy sauce, lemon juice, oil, garlic, ginger, and scallions and mix thoroughly. Brush the mixture on both sides of the chops. Let rest for 30 minutes if possible. Cook the chops for 4–5 minutes per side or until they reach the degree of desired doneness. Makes 4 servings.

Although a delicately charred surface always makes grilled meat taste better, don't forget that sugar and other sweeteners such as the hoisin sauce and honey in this recipe burn easily. Keep an eye on the meat and turn it as necessary to prevent the surface from becoming too blackened.

Grilled Rib Steak with Spice Rub

A plain grilled steak is wonderful but there's more pizzazz when you coat the meat with a rub. You can make the rub mixture (minus the olive oil) in larger quantities and store it in airtight plastic containers. Garlic and Scallion Smashed Potatoes (page 182) or Mustard-Roasted Potatoes with Lemon-Oregano Dressing (page 189) and Herb-Roasted Carrot and Parsnip "Fries" (page 187) are all tasty accompaniments for this dish. Another good side dish would be caramelized Vidalia onions (see the recipe for Bulgur Wheat with Lentils, Caramelized Onions, and Mushrooms, page 67).

> 1 tablespoon chile powder
> 1 teaspoon dried oregano
> ½ teaspoon ground cumin
> ½ teaspoon ground coriander
> ½ teaspoon garlic powder
> ½ teaspoon paprika
> ¼ teaspoon freshly ground black pepper
> 2 tablespoons extra virgin olive oil
> 4 rib steaks, at least 1 inch thick

Preheat the oven broiler or outdoor grill with the rack about 4–6 inches from the heat source (or use a grill pan). Combine the chile powder, oregano, cumin, coriander, garlic powder, paprika, and pepper in a small bowl. Mix ingredients to blend. Add the olive oil and stir until the ingredients are well combined. Rub the mixture on both sides of the steaks. Cook the steaks for about 3 minutes per side or until cooked to desired doneness. Makes 4 servings.

The rub mixture is delicious on chicken, too.

Lamb Chops with Charmoula Pesto

Charmoula is a spicy, pesto-like sauce popular in Moroccan cuisine. This sauce is also a terrific marinade for London broil and chicken, and I've added it with good results to jazz up plain old egg salad, soups, mayonnaise, and salad dressing.

> 3 large garlic cloves, minced
> 2 teaspoons paprika
> 1 teaspoon ground cumin
> ¼ teaspoon cayenne pepper
> ½ cup minced fresh parsley
> ⅓ cup minced fresh cilantro
> ¼ cup lemon juice
> ⅓ cup extra virgin olive oil
> 4 large shoulder lamb chops, ¾–1 inch thick

Preheat the oven broiler or outdoor grill with the rack about 4–6 inches from the heat source (or use a grill pan). Combine the garlic, paprika, cumin, cayenne, parsley, and cilantro in a small bowl. Stir in the lemon juice. Add the olive oil gradually, beating it into the other ingredients. Coat the chops on both sides with the pesto. Let rest for 30 minutes if possible. Cook the chops for 4–5 minutes per side or until they reach the degree of desired doneness. Makes 4 servings.

To make charmoula mayonnaise, **combine ½ cup mayonnaise and 1½–2 teaspoons charmoula.**

Grilled Veal Chops with Sautéed Escarole

I've suggested using shoulder chops for this recipe even though they aren't as tender as rib chops, because shoulder costs so much less (but you can use either). And you can make the dish without the escarole, but mild veal and bitter escarole complement each other so well that I paired them in one recipe. If the escarole finishes first, don't let that worry you. It's a vegetable that's supposed to be wilted and soggy. It balances the crisped meat nicely. Another good side dish for the veal is Easy Beans (page 186).

> 4 shoulder veal chops, about 1 inch thick
> 6 tablespoons extra virgin olive oil
> 2 tablespoons lemon juice
> 1½ teaspoons minced fresh sage or ½ teaspoon dried sage
> Freshly ground black pepper, to taste
> 1½–2 pounds escarole
> 2 medium garlic cloves, minced
> ½ teaspoon red pepper flakes
> Salt, to taste

Preheat an outdoor grill or oven broiler with the rack about 4 inches from the heat source (or use a grill pan). Place the chops in a shallow dish. Mix 2 tablespoons olive oil and the lemon juice and pour over the meat. Sprinkle with the sage and pepper to taste. Turn the meat to coat both sides. Let rest. To prepare the escarole, cut the leaves coarsely into 2-inch pieces and wash them thoroughly. Heat the remaining 4 tablespoons olive oil in a large pan over medium heat. Add the garlic and red pepper flakes and stir briefly, then add the escarole (there may still be droplets of water clinging to the leaves) and start turning the leaves immediately to coat them with olive oil. Add 2 tablespoons water and sprinkle with salt and pepper. Cook, covered, for 4–5 minutes or until the escarole is completely wilted. Remove the cover and cook for 2–3 minutes more, or until the liquid has evaporated from the pan. Place equal amounts of the escarole on each of four plates. Prepare the chops while the escarole is cooking: Cook the meat for about 4 minutes per side or until cooked to desired doneness. Place the chops slightly on top of the vegetable, using the escarole as a bed for the meat. Makes 4 servings.

Use long-handled tongs to turn the escarole and other leafy vegetables.

Grilled Lamb Kebabs with Mustard-Herb Marinade

This almost-classic marinade for lamb gets an extra kick from the fresh lemon peel and cayenne pepper. I change the vegetables depending on what I have in the fridge. I've made these kebabs using shallots, mushrooms, and plum tomatoes that I've cut into chunks. Cooked whole small red bliss potatoes would be fine on the skewers, too.

> 1½ pounds boneless lamb cut into 1½-inch chunks
> ½ cup extra virgin olive oil
> ¼ cup lemon juice
> 1½ tablespoons Dijon mustard
> 2 tablespoons minced fresh chives
> 1 tablespoons minced fresh rosemary (or 1 teaspoon
>   crushed dried rosemary)
> 1 large garlic clove, minced
> ½ teaspoon finely grated fresh lemon peel
> ⅛ teaspoon cayenne pepper
> 2 bay leaves
> 1 red bell pepper, deseeded, cut into 1½-inch chunks
> 6 thick scallions, cut into 1-inch lengths
> 2 narrow small zucchini, cut into 1-inch-thick slices

Put the meat in a nonreactive bowl. Mix together the olive oil, lemon juice, mustard, chives, rosemary, garlic, lemon peel, and cayenne and pour the mixture over the meat. Press the bay leaves into the liquid. Let the meat marinate for 1 hour if possible, stirring occasionally. Brush the vegetables with some of the marinade. Preheat the oven broiler or outdoor grill with the rack about 4 6 inches from the heat source. Broil or grill the kebabs for about 10–15 minutes, turning the skewers occasionally, or until the meat reaches the degree of doneness desired, brushing the meat and vegetables occasionally with some of the marinade. Makes 4 servings.

When using an acid-based marinade, use a glass, ceramic, or stainless-steel dish to hold the meat. These are "nonreactive" materials that will not cause a chemical reaction with the food. Don't use an aluminum pan; the metal will combine with the acid and give the food an off taste and color.

Meatballs in Marinara Sauce

This recipe takes a bit more time than most of the others in this book, but it's perfect for those cold days or weekends when you might want to be inside in the warmth of your kitchen cooking something savory and wonderful for dinner. Simmering tomato sauce has such an inviting smell! Everyone will want to stay in and have dinner together. In a pinch you can make the meatballs and use store-bought sauce—you'll need 5 to 6 cups. Of course, you can also make the sauce in advance, even double or triple the recipe and freeze some for the future. This sauce is also terrific for pasta, without the meatballs.

> 3 tablespoons extra virgin olive oil
> 1 medium onion, chopped
> 8 medium garlic cloves, minced
> 2 (28-ounce) cans Italian plum tomatoes, chopped, with liquid
> ¼ cup minced fresh basil
> Salt and freshly ground black pepper, to taste
> 1½ pounds ground beef or beef and veal
> 2 tablespoons minced fresh parsley
> 2 large eggs
> 1 cup packed fresh bread crumbs

Preheat the oven to 450°F. Heat the olive oil in a large saucepan over low-medium heat and add the onion. Cook for 3 minutes or until the onion has softened. Add four of the minced garlic cloves and cook briefly. Add the tomatoes, 2 tablespoons basil, salt, and pepper to taste. Cook for 30 minutes. While the sauce is cooking, combine the meat, remaining 2 tablespoons basil, parsley, remaining four garlic cloves, and the eggs and mix gently. Add the bread crumbs and mix in gently. Shape the meat into twelve meatballs and place them on a baking sheet. Bake for about 15 minutes, turning them once, until well browned. Add them to the sauce and cook for at least 30 minutes over low heat. Makes 4 servings.

Use a hand blender for the sauce! It will break up the tomatoes right in the pot and give you a smoother sauce.

The reason to mix ground meat gently is to prevent it from becoming overworked, which can make the meatballs (and also burgers and meatloaf) tough and chewy.

Lamb Oreganata

This is a classic way to make lamb. The lemon and oregano, both bold flavors, are equal to lamb's typically assertive taste. It's best to serve this dish with simple vegetables like mashed or Mustard-Roasted Potatoes with Lemon-Oregano Dressing (page 189), Spinach with Garlic, Chile Pepper, and Lemon (page 196), or Roasted Plum Tomatoes (page 191).

> 1½–2 pounds boneless lamb or 4 shoulder
>   lamb chops about 1 inch thick
> ¼ cup lemon juice
> 2 tablespoons extra virgin olive oil
> 1 tablespoon Dijon mustard
> 2 large garlic cloves, minced
> 1½ teaspoons dried oregano
> Salt and freshly ground black pepper, to taste

Place the meat in a nonreactive dish. Combine the lemon juice, olive oil, mustard, garlic, oregano, salt, and pepper and pour over the meat. Let marinate for 1–3 hours. Preheat the oven broiler or outdoor grill with the rack about 4–6 inches from the heat (or use a grill pan). Cook the lamb for about 3–4 minutes per side or until it is cooked to the desired doneness. Makes 4 servings.

Quick Osso Buco

Osso buco is a fragrant, savory dish that's usually made by braising veal shin (shanks) for hours and hours over low heat. My family loves the flavor that results from that long braising, but I don't always have the time to make it that way, so I make this quick version using ground veal. It doesn't have the hearty appeal of meat on the bone, but the flavor is outstanding. Like standard osso buco, this is wonderful when served over risotto or rice, but I usually treat it as meat sauce and put it on top of spaghetti.

2 tablespoons extra virgin olive oil
1 medium onion, chopped
1 stalk celery, chopped
1 medium carrot, chopped
3 garlic cloves, minced
20–24 ounces ground veal
1 (1½-inch) strip lemon peel
½ cup beef stock
½ cup white wine or additional beef stock
2 tomatoes, chopped
2 tablespoons tomato paste
Freshly ground black pepper, to taste
2 teaspoons minced fresh marjoram or oregano

Heat the olive oil in a large sauté pan over medium heat. Add the onion, celery, and carrot and cook for about 3 minutes or until it has softened slightly. Add the garlic and cook briefly. Add the veal and cook for another 3 minutes or until no traces of pink show. Add the lemon peel, stock, wine, tomatoes, tomato paste, pepper, and marjoram or oregano. Bring the ingredients to a simmer. Cover the pan and simmer for 30 minutes. Makes 4 servings.

Rack of Lamb with Lemon-Coriander Crumbs

Rack of lamb is expensive, so it's always a special treat. This is a truly simple recipe for a luxurious and elegant looking dish.

2 racks of lamb
1 tablespoon Dijon mustard
1 tablespoon finely grated fresh lemon peel
1 tablespoon ground coriander
2 large garlic cloves, minced
1 tablespoon minced fresh cilantro
¼ cup fresh bread crumbs

Preheat the oven to 450°F. Place the lamb in a roasting pan. Brush with the mustard. Sprinkle with the lemon peel, coriander, garlic, and cilantro. Scatter the bread crumbs on top. Roast for 25–40 minutes, depending on how well-done you like your meat: a meat thermometer will read 120–125°F for rare and 135–140°F for medium. Let the roast stand about 10 minutes before you serve it. Makes 4–6 servings.

Skirt Steak
with Orange-Chile Marinade and Fruit Salsa

It's a little sweet, a little hot, so every part of your tongue will love this dish. You can make it in the broiler, on your outdoor grill, or even in a grill pan. Two hours is the best marinating time, but, in a pinch, you can give it as little as 30 minutes. The salsa is a cool and refreshing accompaniment that you can prepare a day ahead.

2–2½ pound skirt steak or London broil
⅓ cup orange juice
3 tablespoons bottled chile sauce
2½ tablespoons soy sauce
2½ tablespoons vegetable oil
1 large garlic clove, minced
1 teaspoon sugar
1 teaspoon grated fresh orange peel
¼ teaspoon hot pepper sauce, or to taste

Fruit Salsa

1½ cups diced mango, papaya, or both
1 diced tart apple
⅓ cup chopped red bell pepper
⅓ cup chopped green bell pepper
3 tablespoons rice wine vinegar or white wine vinegar
1½ tablespoons minced fresh cilantro
1½ tablespoons sugar
¼ teaspoon hot pepper sauce, or to taste

Place the meat in a nonreactive dish. In a bowl, combine the orange juice, chile sauce, soy sauce, oil, garlic, 1 teaspoon sugar, orange peel, and ¼ teaspoon hot pepper sauce. Pour the mixture over the meat and let it marinate for at least two hours. If possible, turn the meat once or twice during marinating time. Preheat a broiler or outdoor grill with the rack about 4–6 inches from the heat source (or use a grill pan). Remove the meat from the marinade and wipe the surface lightly with paper toweling. Cook for 2½–4 minutes per side, depending on the degree of doneness desired. Let rest for 5 minutes before carving. Prepare the salsa while the meat marinates, by combining the mango, apple, red bell pepper, green bell pepper, vinegar, cilantro, sugar, and hot pepper sauce in a bowl. Refrigerate the salsa until serving time. Serve the salsa with the grilled meat. Makes 4 servings.

> If you have time, soak the meat in cold water for about 30 minutes to remove some of the salt.

Steak Fajitas

Fajitas are very forgiving. You can grill the meat if you prefer and make it spicier by adding more jalapeño pepper. You can cook the vegetables longer if you like, to caramelize and soften them. Traditionally, fajita fillings are served inside tortillas, but you can eat the meat, vegetables, and bread separately. Same goes for the accompaniments of tomatoes and avocado—they add another dimension to the dish, but you can leave them out if you don't have them in your kitchen or there's no time to get them ready.

1½ pounds fillet split, chuck, skirt, or hanger steak
6 tablespoons lime juice
6 tablespoons extra virgin olive oil
3 large garlic cloves, minced
2 tablespoons minced fresh cilantro
1 teaspoon minced fresh jalapeño pepper
½ teaspoon ground cumin
Freshly ground black pepper, to taste
8 large flour tortillas
2 medium yellow onions, sliced
2 medium yellow or red bell peppers, deseeded and sliced
1 avocado, peeled, pitted, and mashed with some lime or
    lemon juice, optional
2 large tomatoes, chopped, optional

Place the meat in a nonreactive dish. Combine the lime juice, 2 tablespoons olive oil, garlic, cilantro, jalapeño, cumin, and pepper and pour over the meat. Marinate for ½–2 hours. Preheat the oven to 325°F. Wrap the tortillas in aluminum foil and place them in the oven to keep warm. Remove the meat from the marinade. Preheat a heavy sauté pan over medium-high heat. Add 1 tablespoon olive oil. Add the steak and cook for about 3–4 minutes per side or until it reaches the degree of doneness desired. Transfer the meat to a cutting board. Add the remaining 3 tablespoons olive oil to the pan. Add the onions and bell peppers and cook, stirring frequently, for 5–6 minutes or until the vegetables have softened. Carve the meat into thin slices. Place equal amounts of meat over the tortillas and top with the vegetables. Add the accompaniments, if using. Fold the tortillas to enclose the filling. Makes 4 servings.

You can also make fajitas with chicken: use 4 boneless breast halves cut into shreds and cook, stirring occasionally, for 4–5 minutes or until cooked through. To cut the chicken into shreds, place the breasts in the freezer for about 30 minutes, to firm them. Use a sharp chef's knife to cut the breasts into slices, then cut the slices into shreds.

POULTRY

In the "What Does Kosher Mean?" section, I noted the general rules regarding kosher and nonkosher birds. Generally speaking, to make quick and easy meals you'll probably be using cut-up chicken parts such as breasts, thighs, and drumsticks, boneless chicken breasts, duck breast, and turkey breast. Remember that, like meat, kosher poultry is soaked and salted—"brined"—so it is naturally flavorful and juicy. As with all brined ingredients, be judicious with the amount of salt you add to a recipe.

CHICKEN

Chicken is the basic black of foods. You can use it over and over in any season, serve it plain or dress it up with a sauce, salsa, relish, or crust. It never gets boring because it is so remarkably versatile. Use it whole or just its parts; sauté it, braise it, or cook it on a grill. The meat is so delicately flavored that just a pinch of exotic saffron or a few sprigs of fragrant dill will do wonders for it, as you'll see when you prepare Chicken Soup without the Soup (page 127). But you can also be bold with chicken. The same mild flesh goes deliciously with assertive ingredients such as chile powder and mustard, robust wine- or vinegar-based dressings, and even the sweet, warm flavors of cinnamon and dried fruit called for in the recipe for Pan-Roasted Persian-Spiced Chicken with Fruited Rice (page 128).

While all this is enough to make chicken an American favorite, there's more. This bird is easy to cook and, with the right recipes, you can be out of the kitchen and sitting at the table in no time.

Whenever a recipe calls for a cut-up broiler-fryer chicken you can substitute separate parts: 4 breasts plus wings or 4 whole legs (including thigh plus drumstick), or 8 large drumsticks or 8 large thighs.

Some recipes in this book call for cooking chicken to specific internal temperatures. The USDA recommends cooking chicken to 165°F, however, to maintain juiciness, many cooks remove chicken from the heat when a meat thermometer registers 160°F (the temperature will rise a few degrees after it is removed from the heat). Each person must make the decision as to whether to use the more conservative guidelines. In any case, use a meat thermometer, standard or instant read, to check the internal temperature of the meat.

TURKEY

Turkey used to be a once-a-year dish, but many people no longer wait for Thanksgiving to enjoy it for dinner. Although a large roasted bird with juicy meat and golden brown skin continues to impress as the ultimate holiday meal, it's easier and quicker to use turkey parts during the rest of the year. Turkey breasts, whole, halved, and boneless, are widely available, ready for you to prepare Mustard-Honey Roasted Turkey Breast (page 138) or Roasted Turkey Breast with Chutney and Pears (page 141). Some stores sell "turkey London broil," a half, boneless turkey breast, which is great for grilling with Chipotle Pesto (page 137). Turkey cutlets are a godsend when you want a quick dinner; they cook in almost no time and are amazingly versatile: marinate and grill them or pan-fry them with a light bread crumb coating or, if you prefer something easy but more glamorous, try them as Turkey Paillards with Balsamic Sauce (page 144). Ground turkey makes magnificent chilethat's lower in fat than the standard version made with beef.

As with chicken, there are some extra considerations when it comes to turkey breast. The USDA recommends cooking it to an internal temperature of 170°F, but many cooks find that too high to produce juicy meat and instead remove a turkey breast from the oven when a meat thermometer registers 160°F. Again, as with chicken, you must decide whether to use the more conservative guidelines. In any case, use a meat thermometer, standard or instant read, to check the internal temperature of the meat.

CORNISH HENS AND DUCK

Chicken and turkey are the workhorses of many American kitchens. But when day-to-day dinners become humdrum, Cornish hens and duck make good alternatives. Cornish hens are small chickens, usually weighing just over one pound and serving two people. You can season and treat them just as you would chicken. For quick cooking, split them down the middle; they'll grill or broil through in 25 minutes.

Duck is a bolder, gamier bird with a bountiful flavor that's a treat from time to time. As with chicken and turkey, you can buy separated duck parts. The breast portion is particularly accommodating because it is lean and cooks quickly.

Both Cornish hens and duck make attractive presentations on a plate, making these birds especially suitable for company.

POULTRY

✓ A bird species is kosher if it has been considered so by tradition and is not one of the 24 forbidden species mentioned in the Bible.

✓ Kosher poultry can include chicken, Cornish hen, turkey, goose, and duck.

✓ There is some disagreement as to whether quail, squab, dove, and pheasant are kosher.

✓ Birds of prey are among the prohibited species.

✓ Ritual slaughter must be performed by a professional (shochet).

✓ Kosher poultry is soaked and salted to eliminate prohibited blood.

CHICKEN

Barbecued Boneless Chicken Breasts
with Quick Corn Relish

The basting sauce in this recipe is HOT! But you can cut down on the red pepper flakes if you prefer it less spicy. You can make the sauce up to 4 days ahead and use it for grilled turkey, veal, or hamburgers. Corn goes so well with this dish: if it's summer, make corn on the cob. In other seasons, rely on frozen kernels and turn them into a quick corn relish.

> 2 tablespoons extra virgin olive oil
> 1 medium onion, minced
> 1 garlic clove, minced
> ½ teaspoon red pepper flakes
> 1 (8-ounce) can tomato sauce
> ¼ cup apple cider vinegar
> 1 tablespoon Worcestershire sauce
> ¼ cup brown sugar
> 2 ½ teaspoons chile powder
> 2 teaspoons ground cumin
> ½ teaspoon chipotle powder
> 1 teaspoon mustard powder
> 4–6 boneless and skinless chicken breast halves

Preheat an outdoor grill or oven broiler with the rack about 6 inches from the heat source. Heat the olive oil in a saucepan over medium heat. Add the onion, garlic, and red pepper flakes. Cook for 2–3 minutes or until the vegetables have softened. Add the tomato sauce, ⅓ cup water, vinegar, Worcestershire sauce, sugar, chile powder, cumin, chipotle powder, and mustard powder. Stir ingredients, bring the mixture to a boil and turn the heat to low-medium. Cook for about 20 minutes or until sauce thickens to a syrupy texture. Broil or grill the chicken for 2–6 minutes per side, depending on thickness, or until they are cooked through, turning pieces once or twice and brushing them frequently with the sauce. Makes 4 servings.

Quick Corn Relish

2 tablespoons extra virgin olive oil
4 thick scallions, chopped
½ red bell pepper, chopped, optional
1 (10-ounce) package frozen corn kernels, thawed
2 tablespoons minced fresh parsley
Salt and freshly ground black pepper, to taste

Heat the olive oil in a sauté pan over medium heat. Add the scallions and optional bell pepper and cook for 2 minutes. Add the corn, parsley, and salt and pepper to taste and cook for about 2 minutes, stirring often, until the corn is heated through. Makes 4 servings.

Most Worcestershire sauces contain anchovies, and a kosher regulation prohibits mixing of meat and fish in the same dish. However, if the amount of fish is less than 1.66 percent of all ingredients, the fish is considered "nullified." For use with meat, be aware of products that contain fish. OU, one of the kosher certifying agencies, labels products OU "Fish" when the product contains more than 1.66 percent fish. Alternatively, you can use vegetarian Worcestershire sauce or substitute soy sauce.

Pan-Roasted Lemon-Garlic Chicken

Pan roasting lets you enjoy the taste and texture of crispy-crusted, roasted food in much less time than traditional roasting. The simple taste of Lemon-Garlic Chicken goes perfectly with Sautéed Escarole (page 108) and mashed potatoes or Pan-Fried Paprika Potatoes (page 192).

> 1 broiler-fryer chicken, cut into 8 parts
> 2 tablespoons extra virgin olive oil
> 6 tablespoons lemon juice
> 1 tablespoon Dijon mustard
> 2 garlic cloves, minced
> 1 tablespoon minced fresh oregano (or 1 teaspoon
>   dried oregano)
> Freshly ground black pepper, to taste
> 1 large onion, sliced

Preheat the oven to 425°F. Rinse and dry the chicken parts. Heat the olive oil in a large sauté pan over medium-high heat and cook the chicken, turning the pieces occasionally, for about 8 minutes or until the skin is browned. Remove the pan from the heat. Combine the lemon juice, mustard, garlic, and oregano in a small bowl. Whisk the ingredients until they are well blended. Pour the dressing over the chicken. Sprinkle with pepper to taste. Add the onion to the pan, placing the slices around the chicken. Place the pan in the oven. Roast for about 12–16 minutes, or until chicken is cooked through. Place the chicken on a serving platter, spoon contents of the pan on top and serve. Makes 4 servings.

A meat thermometer is the only really reliable way to check if food is cooked to the desired doneness. There are several types:

- ⸙ In a traditional probe model the probe is inserted at least 2 inches into the meat and typically stays in the roast throughout cooking.

- ⸙ An oven-cord probe model lets you check the temperature of food without opening the oven door. The probe goes into the food and is attached on the other end to a long metal wire; the wire is inserted inside a digital thermometer base unit that sits on a counter or, if magnetized, onto the oven door; an alarm sounds when the preset temperature has been reached. There are newer "wireless" models that transmit temperature readings and alarm sounds from the probe to a remote, untethered handset.

- ⸙ An instant-read thermometer is not designed to stay in the food or the oven. It is inserted toward the end of cooking time. Most are inserted only ½ inch into the food to get an accurate reading, making these especially good for burgers and chicken breasts.

- ⸙ Thermometer forks are instant-read thermometers that are attached to the end of a long two-pronged fork. They measure even the thinnest foods and are particularly good when grilling thin cutlets, chops, and the like.

Chicken in the Pot with Pears, Dried Figs, and Cider

This is a perfect dish for autumn, when apple cider is fresh. Because there will be savory juices when the dish is fully cooked, it pairs well with rice, couscous, or egg noodles. Add a green vegetable such as sautéed spinach (or Spinach with Garlic, Chile Pepper, and Lemon, page 196) to round out the meal. Parsnip and Potato Puree (page 195) is another good option.

> 1 broiler-fryer chicken, cut into 8 parts
> 2 tablespoons vegetable oil
> 1 large shallot, chopped
> 2 teaspoons minced fresh ginger
> 6 chopped dried figs
> ¼ cup golden raisins
> 1 tablespoon curry powder
> ⅛ teaspoon cayenne pepper
> ⅔ cups apple cider or home-style apple juice
> 2 pears, peeled, cored, and cut into large chunks

Rinse and dry the chicken parts. Heat the vegetable oil in a large sauté pan over medium heat and cook the chicken, turning the pieces occasionally, for about 8 minutes, or until the skin is lightly browned. Transfer the chicken to a dish. Discard all but a film of fat from the pan. Add the shallot, ginger, figs, and raisins and cook for 1–2 minutes. Return the chicken and accumulated juices to the pan. Sprinkle it all with curry powder and cayenne. Pour in the cider. Turn the chicken pieces to coat them with the pan juices. Cover the pan, turn the heat to low-medium, and cook for 20 minutes. Add the pears and cook about 5 minutes or until the chicken is cooked through. Makes 4 servings.

> To avoid spattering, be sure the chicken skin is completely dry before adding it to the oil in the pan.
>
> When sautéing chicken, leave space between the pieces so that they brown properly. Use a large pan or cook the chicken parts in batches.

Chicken with Mushrooms and Tomatoes

This entrée has plenty of rich, fragrant gravy! Serve it with polenta or pasta and a bright green vegetable such as broccoli rabe, spinach, or broccoli.

1 broiler-fryer chicken, cut into 8 parts
2 tablespoons extra virgin olive oil
2 onions, sliced
10 ounces fresh white or wild mushrooms
2 garlic cloves, minced
3 tablespoons minced fresh parsley
2 tablespoons minced fresh basil
Freshly ground black pepper, to taste
1 (28-ounce) can Italian-style tomatoes, drained
    and coarsely chopped
½ cup red wine or chicken stock

Rinse and dry the chicken parts. Heat the olive oil in a large sauté pan over medium heat and cook the chicken, turning the pieces occasionally, for about 8 minutes or until the skin is browned. Transfer the chicken to a dish. Discard all but a film of fat from the pan. Add the onions and mushrooms and cook for about 4 minutes or until the vegetables have softened. Add the garlic and stir briefly. Return the chicken and accumulated juices to the pan. Place the vegetables on top of the chicken. Sprinkle the ingredients with the parsley, basil, and pepper to taste. Add the tomatoes and wine or stock and bring to a boil. Cover the pan, turn heat to low-medium and cook for about 25 minutes, basting 3 to 4 times, or until chicken is cooked through. Makes 4 servings.

Canned tomatoes have lots of juice. Even after you drain them, more juices will accumulate. That's okay—you can add that to the sauce.

Chicken Soup without the Soup

Chicken soup has long been a mainstay of kosher cooking. But it takes hours to cook! This dish has the warmth, fragrance, and soothing comforts of homemade chicken soup, but takes much less time, and because it's served with cooked white rice or egg noodles, it has all the elements of a complete dinner.

> 1 broiler-fryer chicken, cut into 8 parts
> 4–6 medium carrots, peeled
> 2 medium parsnips, peeled
> 2 medium stalks celery, strings removed
> 2 tablespoons vegetable oil
> 1 large yellow onion, sliced
> 6 sprigs fresh dill
> ¾ cup chicken stock
> Freshly ground black pepper, to taste
> Cooked white rice or egg noodles

Rinse and dry the chicken parts. Cut the carrots, parsnips, and celery into large chunks. Heat the vegetable oil in a large sauté pan over medium heat and cook the onion, carrots, parsnips, and celery for 2–3 minutes, stirring once or twice. Add the chicken and place the vegetables and dill on top. Pour in the stock and bring to a boil. Cover the pan, turn heat to low-medium, and cook for about 30 minutes, basting 3–4 times, or until chicken is cooked through. Season to taste with pepper. Serve the chicken and vegetables over the rice or egg noodles. Pour the pan juices on top. Makes 4 servings.

If you peel the celery, it won't be stringy and will be easier to digest. Use a potato peeler, starting at the wider end of the rib.

Pan-Roasted Persian-Spiced Chicken
with Fruited Rice

This dish is a good choice for dinner in early autumn, when you can buy bountifully flavored, and crisp, freshly picked new-crop apples. The Fruited Rice in this recipe goes well with lots of poultry dishes but it tastes especially good with this one because the tart fruit complements the fragrant spices used on the chicken. To save time you can make the rice ahead and rewarm it.

4 bone-in chicken breast halves or whole legs
2 tablespoons extra virgin olive oil
Freshly ground black pepper, to taste
¼ teaspoon ground cinnamon
¼ teaspoon freshly grated nutmeg
¼ teaspoon ground allspice or ⅛ teaspoon ground cloves
⅛ teaspoon cayenne pepper

Preheat the oven to 425°F. Rinse and dry the chicken parts. Heat the olive oil in a sauté pan over medium-high heat and cook the chicken, turning pieces once, for about 8 minutes, or until the skin is browned. Sprinkle the chicken with pepper, cinnamon, nutmeg, and allspice. Place the pan in the oven. Roast for about 12–16 minutes, or until chicken is cooked through (an instant-read thermometer should read 160°F). Place chicken on a platter and serve with Fruited Rice. Makes 4 servings.

Fruited Rice

3 tablespoons vegetable oil

1 medium onion, chopped

1 stalk celery, chopped

2 cups cool cooked rice

1 tart apple, peeled, cored, and chopped

1 cup chopped mixed dried fruit such as apricots, raisins,
   figs, or prunes

¼ cup chopped almonds, lightly toasted

½ teaspoon salt, or to taste

1½ teaspoons fresh thyme leaves

Preheat the oven to 425°F. Heat the vegetable oil in an ovenproof sauté pan over medium heat. Add the onion and celery and cook for 2–3 minutes or until slightly softened. Remove the pan from the heat. Add the rice, apple, dried fruit, almonds, salt, and thyme. Mix ingredients thoroughly. Bake for 12–15 minutes or until hot and lightly crispy. Makes about 3½ cups.

It's easier to use cold leftover rice.
Hot rice grains tend to stick together.

Although you can use any kind of apple that appeals to your taste buds, I've suggested tart apples because they have a more vibrant, crisp quality than sweet varieties. Granny Smiths are a widely available tart apple species. Macouns and McIntosh are also good choices. If you live near a farm or farmers' market, you might be lucky enough to find old-fashioned apples such as Staymans and Winesaps, which are fabulously rich, juicy, and perfect for this recipe.

Chicken with Dates and Toasted Almonds

Middle Eastern cooking is replete with recipes that include dates and nuts. This intriguing dish adds honey and hot and spicy Quick Ras el Hanout (page 227), a fragrant blend of spices popular in Morocco. There's a good balance of soft and crunchy, heat and sweet. Steamed couscous would be the perfect accompaniment, plus a green vegetable.

> 1 tablespoon finely chopped almonds, optional
> 4 bone-in chicken breast halves or whole legs or 1 broiler-
>   fryer chicken, cut into 8 parts
> 2 tablespoons extra virgin olive oil
> 1 large onion, chopped
> 2 large garlic cloves, minced
> 1 teaspoon Quick Ras el Hanout
> 1 bay leaf
> 1½ cups chicken stock
> 12–16 dates, pitted and halved
> 2 tablespoons honey

There are many varieties of dates. Any kind will do but Medjools are moist and meaty and they're divinely delicious, so they would be first choice for this recipe. And dates are good for you—rich with fiber and potassium.

Preheat the oven or toaster oven to 400°F and roast the almonds for 5–6 minutes or until they are lightly browned and fragrant. Set aside. Rinse and dry the chicken parts. Heat the olive oil in a large sauté pan over medium heat and cook the chicken, turning the pieces occasionally, for about 8 minutes or until the skin is lightly browned. Transfer the chicken to a dish. Discard all but a film of fat from the pan. Add the onion and cook for about 2 minutes or until softened slightly. Add the garlic, Ras el Hanout, bay leaf, and chicken stock and cook over medium-high heat for about 4 minutes or until the liquid has reduced to about one cup. Return the chicken to the pan. Coat the chicken with the pan fluids by turning the pieces once or twice. Cover the pan, turn the heat to low-medium, and cook for about 25 minutes or until cooked through. Transfer the chicken to a serving platter and keep warm. Add the dates and honey to the pan. Cook over medium-high heat for 3–4 minutes or until the sauce has thickened and appears syrupy. Spoon the sauce around and on top of the chicken. Sprinkle with the almonds, if using. Makes 4 servings.

Broiled Chicken with Bread Crumbs and Chile Oil

This hearty dish looks tame but has a kick, thanks to the hot chile oil. The bread crumbs give a pleasantly crispy finish to the tender chicken. Good side dishes include Roasted Plum Tomatoes (page 191), Roasted Asparagus (page 190), Herb-Roasted Carrot and Parsnip "Fries" (page 187), or Green Beans with Lime Butter (page 183).

1 cup fresh bread crumbs
2 tablespoons minced fresh parsley
⅛ teaspoon cayenne pepper
6 tablespoons vegetable oil
1 tablespoon spicy prepared mustard
2 teaspoons lemon juice
1 teaspoon Worcestershire sauce
1 large garlic clove, minced
1 broiler-fryer chicken, cut into 8 parts
2 teaspoons hot chile oil

Preheat the oven broiler with the rack about 6 inches from the heat source. Mix the bread crumbs, parsley, cayenne, 4 tablespoons vegetable oil, mustard, lemon juice, Worcestershire sauce, and garlic in a bowl and set aside. Rinse and dry the chicken parts and place the pieces skin-side down in a broiling pan. Combine the remaining 2 tablespoons vegetable oil and hot chile oil and brush the chicken with this mixture. Broil for 20 minutes, turning the pieces occasionally and basting with the pan fluids. Place the chicken skin side up and press the bread crumb mixture on top. Broil for about 5 minutes or until the coating looks crunchy and golden brown and the chicken is cooked through. Makes 4 servings.

Food can be kept warm with an aluminum foil cover or by placing it in a preheated 140°F oven.

Sautéed Chicken Breasts with Tomatoes and Honey

The gently sweet sauce in this dish, with its tomatoes, honey, and cinnamon, combines flavors familiar in the Middle East. The dish is mild and pleasing and goes nicely with steamed couscous, rice, or polenta.

        4 tablespoons vegetable oil
        4 boneless and skinless chicken breast halves
        1 large onion, chopped
        3 carrots, thinly sliced
        1 garlic clove, minced
        4 medium tomatoes, chopped
        1 tablespoon lemon juice
        1 tablespoon honey
        ¼ teaspoon ground cinnamon
        ⅛ teaspoon ground coriander
        Freshly ground black pepper, to taste

Preheat the oven to 200°F. Heat 2 tablespoons vegetable oil in a sauté pan over medium heat and cook the chicken for 2–6 minutes per side, depending on thickness, or until they are cooked through. Place the chicken breasts on a dish and keep them warm in the oven. Add the remaining 2 tablespoons vegetable oil to the pan and cook the onion and carrot for 2 minutes or until the vegetables have softened but are still crunchy. Add the garlic, tomatoes, lemon juice, honey, cinnamon, and coriander. Cook for about 3–4 minutes. Season to taste with pepper. Spoon the sauce onto plates, place chicken on top and serve. Makes 4 servings.

Grilled Marinated Chicken Breasts
with Bruschetta

This is a recipe that I make again and again because grilled chicken breasts are a cinch to prepare and can take under 30 minutes. They are also so basic that you can change the recipe any number of ways to suit yourself. For example, I often use olive oil instead of vegetable oil, and lemon juice in place of vinegar. I also vary the herb, switching from rosemary to oregano or thyme. I make this dish for company and if someone is a dark-meat eater, I'll include boneless thighs (but increase the cooking time by 3 to 4 minutes). Grilled boneless chicken is suitable as a dinner entrée, served with side dishes, but you can also stuff the meat into a sandwich or carve it into strips to place over greens. The dish is fine plain, but I like to add a relish or salad of some sort to give it more flavor and enhanced texture. Bruschetta is easy enough so it's my go-to accompaniment on a busy day.

> 4 boneless and skinless chicken breast halves
> 2 tablespoons vegetable oil
> 2 tablespoons red wine vinegar
> 2 teaspoons Dijon mustard
> 1 shallot, chopped
> 1 garlic clove, minced
> 2 teaspoons fresh thyme leaves (or use ½ teaspoon dried thyme)
> Freshly ground black pepper, to taste

Place the chicken in a nonreactive dish. Combine the oil, vinegar, mustard, shallot, garlic, thyme, and pepper in a small bowl. Whisk the ingredients until they are well blended. Pour the dressing over the chicken and marinate for 15–60 minutes. If possible, turn the chicken once or twice during this time. Preheat an outdoor grill or oven broiler with the rack about 6 inches from the heat source (or use a grill pan). Remove the chicken from the marinade and cook the pieces for 2–6 minutes per side, depending on thickness, or until they are cooked through. Makes 4 servings.

Thin (¼-inch) cutlets will be done after about 2 minutes per side, but larger, thicker ones will take longer. You can make thick breasts thinner by slicing them in half crosswise or by pounding them with a meat mallet or the flat bottom of a heavy pot. Pounding the breasts will also even them out so they can cook more uniformly. To do this, place the breasts on a cutting board between pieces of waxed or parchment paper. Strike the chicken breasts with a meat mallet (or pot bottom) until they are about ½ inch thick.

Bruschetta

Bruschetta is usually an hors d'oeuvre made with garlic toast rounds topped with various ingredients such as chopped plum tomatoes. Because plum tomatoes have thick skins, most people peel them, which takes extra time, but I always use grape tomatoes, so I skip this step. Bruschetta is a terrific topping for grilled chicken and the contrast of hot meat and cool salad is a delight for the palate.

> 1 pint grape tomatoes
> 3 tablespoons extra virgin olive oil
> 2 garlic cloves, minced
> 3 tablespoons minced fresh basil
> Large pinch of cayenne pepper
> Salt, to taste

Cut the grape tomatoes into quarters and place them in a bowl. Add the olive oil, garlic, basil, cayenne, and salt to taste. Mix gently. Makes about 2 cups.

Marinades are used to give flavor to ingredients. But meats and poultry left too long in an acidic marinade can become mushy or even tough. Marinate the meat only long enough to absorb flavor. Remember that poultry is perishable, so be sure to keep it in the refrigerator while it rests in the marinade.

Pan-Roasted Chicken
with Lemon, Olives, Capers, and Rosemary

If you like pungent, highly flavorful foods, you'll enjoy this dish. Try to use cured green and black olives. You can find them in the deli sections of specialty markets and many supermarkets; otherwise, use tangy Mediterranean-style varieties from a jar. Milder canned black olives don't offer the same depth of flavor. Plain white rice or mashed potatoes and sautéed spinach, chard, or other winter greens would be good accompaniments.

4 bone-in chicken breast halves or whole legs
   (thigh plus drumstick)
2 tablespoons extra virgin olive oil
1 onion, chopped
2 garlic cloves, minced
2 lemons, sliced
1 tablespoon capers, rinsed
1 tablespoon minced fresh rosemary
½ cup pitted green olives, cut in half
½ cup cured pitted black and green olives, cut in half

Preheat the oven to 425°F. Rinse and dry the chicken. Heat the olive oil in an ovenproof sauté pan over medium-high heat and cook the chicken, turning pieces occasionally, for about 8 minutes or until the skin is browned. Transfer the chicken to a dish. Discard all but a film of fat from the pan and turn heat to medium. Add the onion to the pan and cook for 2–3 minutes or until softened. Add the garlic and cook briefly. Return the chicken and accumulated juices to the pan. Add the lemon slices, capers, rosemary, and olives. Place the pan in the oven. Roast for about 12–16 minutes, or until chicken is cooked through (an instant-read thermometer should read 160°F). Place chicken on a serving platter, spoon contents of the pan on top and serve. Makes 4 servings.

Sautéed Chicken Breasts
with Avocado and Tomato

You can prepare this dish ahead of time and pop it into the oven to reheat just before serving. A large habanero pepper will make this dish quite spicy. But if you prefer less heat cut down on the amount or use a less fiery pepper (see the sidebar in the recipe for Tomato-Avocado Salad, page 63).

⅓ cup all-purpose flour
Freshly ground black pepper, to taste
½ teaspoon ground cumin
4 boneless and skinless chicken breast halves, about ½
    inch thick
3 tablespoons extra virgin olive oil
⅓ cup chopped red onion
1 medium avocado, peeled, pitted, and cut into bite-size chunks
2 tomatoes, cut into bite-size pieces
1 habanero pepper, deseeded and minced

Preheat the oven to 375°F. Mix the flour, pepper, and cumin in a dish. Dredge the chicken in the mixture and shake to remove the excess. Heat the olive oil in a sauté pan over medium heat and cook the chicken for 3–4 minutes per side or until lightly crispy. Place the chicken in a baking dish. Cover with the onion, avocado, and tomatoes. Scatter the habanero pepper on top. Bake for 6–8 minutes or until chicken is cooked through and the vegetables have softened. Makes 4 servings.

This recipe can be made using 1¼–1½ pounds of turkey cutlets. Turkey cutlets are thinner than chicken breasts, so sauté them for a shorter amount of time, about 2 minutes per side.

TURKEY

Boneless Broiled Turkey
London Broil with Chipotle Pesto

This is a spicy dish! You can use this as is—Sautéed Carrots with Mint and Shallots (page 194) is a refreshing partner for it—but I like to serve it as a salad: cut the broiled meat into slices and put them on top of lettuce, tomato, and cucumber salad (drizzle with vinaigrette). The meat also makes a terrific sandwich filler: spread some crusty bread with mayo lightened with a bit of fresh lime or lemon juice.

> 1 small onion, coarsely cut
> 2 large garlic cloves, quartered
> 2 tablespoons minced fresh cilantro
> ¼ cup canned chipotle peppers in adobo
> 5 tablespoons extra virgin olive oil
> 1 teaspoon chile powder
> 1 teaspoon ground cumin
> 1 teaspoon paprika
> ½ teaspoon dried oregano
> 1½ pounds turkey London broil

Preheat an outdoor grill or oven broiler with the rack about 6 inches from the heat source. To make the pesto, place the onion, garlic, cilantro, chipotle peppers, 4 tablespoons olive oil, chile powder, cumin, paprika, and oregano in a food processor and process until pureed. Brush the turkey with the remaining tablespoon olive oil. Broil for about 15 minutes, turning the meat 2–3 times. Brush some of the pesto on the turkey and cook for about 20–25 minutes, turning the meat occasionally and brushing with the remaining pesto, or until it is cooked through. Let rest for 10 minutes before serving. Makes 4 servings.

Mustard-Honey Roasted Turkey Breast

Although this recipe doesn't take long to prepare, it takes longer to cook, so it's a good choice for the weekend, when there's more time to wait for dinner. It's also fine for Thanksgiving if you don't want the fuss and bother of a whole turkey. I like to serve this with the Cranberry-Orange Sauce from the recipe for Challah French Toast (page 157) or Herb-Roasted Carrot and Parsnip "Fries" (page 187), Sautéed Brussels Sprouts with Onions (page 193), or Stir-Fried Fennel (page 198).

1 bone-in half turkey breast, about 2½ pounds
2 tablespoons Dijon mustard
2 tablespoons extra virgin olive oil
2 tablespoons honey
1½ teaspoons finely grated fresh orange peel
1½ teaspoons minced fresh rosemary (or ½ teaspoon dried
    rosemary)
Freshly ground black pepper, to taste
1 cup orange juice

Preheat the oven to 425°F. Rinse and dry the turkey breast and place it skin side up in a roasting pan. Combine the mustard, olive oil, honey, orange peel, rosemary, and black pepper to taste. Brush the mixture on the turkey. Roast for 25 minutes and pour in the orange juice. Reduce the heat to 350°F. Continue to roast for about 35–45 minutes basting occasionally with the pan juices or until the meat is cooked through and a meat thermometer inserted into the thickest part reads 160–170°F. Let rest for 15 minutes before carving. Serve with the pan juices separately. Makes 4 servings.

Because they are so sturdy and flexible, silicone brushes are a terrific and easy way to brush thick glazes, basting sauces, and condiments onto poultry or meat. They are also dishwasher safe.

Lime and Macadamia Nut–Crusted
Turkey Cutlets with Tropical Salsa

Macadamias are rich and they give terrific crunch; the salsa in this recipe (you can make it a day or so ahead) is tangy and soft, so there's good balance in this dish. I've made the salsa without the turkey and served it as a dip for chips.

> 1½–2 pounds turkey cutlets
> 2 tablespoons lime juice
> 2 tablespoons extra virgin olive oil
> 1 teaspoon Dijon mustard
> Pinch of cayenne pepper
> 1 cup finely chopped macadamias
> 4–5 tablespoons vegetable oil

Place the cutlets in a nonreactive dish. Mix the 2 tablespoons lime juice, 2 tablespoons olive oil, mustard, and cayenne and pour over the turkey. Let marinate 10–20 minutes. Turn the turkey once or twice during this time. Coat the turkey with the macadamias, pressing the nuts onto the meat. Let rest for 5 minutes. Heat 4 tablespoons vegetable oil in a sauté pan over medium heat. Cook the turkey for about 2–3 minutes per side or until golden brown and crispy, adding more vegetable oil if needed to prevent sticking. Drain on paper towels and serve with the salsa.

Tropical Salsa

> 2 mangoes, peeled and diced
> 1 avocado, peeled and diced
> 1 jalapeño pepper, deseeded and minced
> ⅓ cup chopped red onion
> 2 tablespoons minced fresh cilantro or flat-leaf parsley
> ½ teaspoon finely grated fresh lime peel
> 1 medium garlic clove, minced
> 3 tablespoons lime juice
> 1 tablespoon extra virgin olive oil

Combine the mangoes, avocado, jalapeño, onion, cilantro, lime peel, and garlic and toss ingredients gently. Mix in the 3 tablespoons lime juice and 1 tablespoon olive oil. Set aside.

Pomegranate-Glazed Turkey London Broil

Turkey London broil is another name for a half skinless and boneless turkey breast. It's lean and luscious meat, but because there's no skin or fat to keep it moist, it's best to baste the meat or give it a moisturizing glaze or sauce. This one, made with pomegranate paste and orange marmalade is tangy, but sweet too. Try this dish with Sweet Potato Pancakes (page 199).

> ¼ cup pomegranate paste
> 2 tablespoons sweet orange marmalade
> 1 tablespoon minced fresh ginger
> 1 teaspoon Dijon mustard
> ½ teaspoon finely grated fresh lime peel
> 1½ pounds turkey London broil
> 2 teaspoons extra virgin olive oil
> Freshly ground black pepper, to taste

Preheat an outdoor grill or oven broiler with the rack about 6 inches from the heat source. Mix the pomegranate paste, orange marmalade, ginger, mustard, and lime peel in a small bowl. Separate and reserve 2 tablespoons of the glaze. Brush the London broil with the olive oil and sprinkle with pepper. Broil for 15 minutes, turning the meat 2–3 times. Brush some of the glaze on the turkey and cook for about 20–25 minutes, turning the meat occasionally and brushing with all but the reserved glaze, or until it is cooked through. Remove from the oven and brush with the reserved glaze. Let rest for 10 minutes before serving. Pour the pan juices over the meat if desired, for extra flavor and juiciness. Makes 4 servings.

> You can use this pomegranate glaze for other kinds of poultry such as roasted chicken, whole turkey, and duck breast.

Roasted Turkey Breast with Chutney and Pears

Everyone in my family loves roasted turkey, so I even cook this dish during the summer (using fresh peaches). The tangy chutney brings out turkey's sweet qualities. Good accompaniments are steamed basmati rice and a simple green vegetable such as sautéed spinach or string beans. Parsnip and Potato Purée (page 195) and Sweet Potato Pancakes (page 199) are other suitable accompaniments.

> 1 boneless or bone-in half turkey breast,
>   about 2½ pounds
> 2 teaspoons extra virgin olive oil
> Freshly ground black pepper, to taste
> ⅓ cup Major Grey's chutney
> 1 teaspoon minced fresh ginger
> ¾ teaspoon curry powder
> 1 tablespoon lime juice
> ½ cup chicken stock
> 4 firm but ripe pears, peeled, cored, and cut into quarters

Preheat the oven to 425°F. Rinse and dry the turkey and place it skin side up in a roasting pan. Brush the skin with olive oil and sprinkle to taste with pepper. Roast for 25 minutes. Mix the chutney, ginger, curry powder, and lime juice together. When the turkey has roasted for 25 minutes, reduce the heat to 350°F. Spoon the chutney mixture over the meat and spread it evenly. Roast for another 15 minutes and pour the stock and pears into the pan. Roast for another 20–30 minutes, basting occasionally with the pan juices or until the meat is cooked through and a meat thermometer inserted into the thickest part reads 160–170°F. Let rest for 15 minutes before carving. Serve the turkey with the pears and pan juices. Makes 4 servings.

Turkey or Chicken Chili

When I can't think of anything to make for dinner I often turn to this recipe. It's a good rib-sticking dish for a cold winter evening (but I make it throughout the year). You can make this a day or so ahead; in fact, some people prefer the flavor of two-day old chile because the ingredients and flavors have had time to blend and mellow. For a more filling meal, serve it over cooked white or brown rice.

2 tablespoons extra virgin olive oil
1 medium onion, chopped
3 garlic cloves, minced
16–20 ounces ground turkey or chicken
3 large tomatoes, chopped or 1 (28-ounce) can Italian-
     style tomatoes, drained and coarsely chopped
1 (15-ounce) can tomato sauce
2 teaspoons Worcestershire sauce
2 tablespoons chile powder
1 teaspoon ground cumin
1 teaspoon dried oregano
¼ teaspoon red pepper flakes
1 (16-ounce) can red kidney or black beans, drained

Heat the olive oil in a large sauté pan over medium heat. Add the onion and cook for about 3 minutes or until it has softened slightly. Add the garlic and cook briefly. Add the turkey and cook for another 3 minutes or until no traces of pink show. Add the tomatoes, tomato sauce, Worcestershire sauce, chile powder, cumin, oregano, and red pepper flakes. Stir to combine the ingredients. Cover the pan, reduce heat to low-medium, and cook for 30 minutes. Add the beans and cook uncovered for 10 minutes, or until the sauce is thick. Makes 4 servings.

Roasted Turkey Breast
with Balsamic Vinegar Glaze and Sugar Snap Peas

This dish is delicious with Sweet Potato Pancakes (page 199) and a simple sautéed green vegetable such as sugar snap peas.

> 1 bone-in half turkey breast, about 2½ pounds
> 2 teaspoons extra virgin olive oil
> Freshly ground black pepper, to taste
> ½ cup apple cider or home-style apple juice
> ½ cup balsamic vinegar
> 2 tablespoons maple syrup
> 1 teaspoon minced fresh rosemary

Preheat the oven to 425°F. Rinse and dry the turkey breast and place it skin-side up in a roasting pan. Brush the skin with olive oil and sprinkle to taste with pepper. Roast for 25 minutes. While the turkey roasts, combine the apple cider, vinegar, and maple syrup in a small pan. Bring to a boil and cook on high heat for about 10 minutes or until reduced to a syrupy texture. Set aside. When the turkey has roasted for 25 minutes, reduce the oven heat to 350°F. Brush some of the vinegar mixture on the breast and sprinkle with rosemary. Roast for another 15 minutes and brush with the remaining glaze. Continue to roast for another 20–30 minutes or until a meat thermometer placed in the thickest part of the breast measures 160–170°F, basting occasionally with the pan juices. Remove the turkey from the oven and let rest for about 15 minutes before carving. Serve with pan fluids. Makes 4 servings.

> It's a cinch to make sautéed sugar snaps: wash and trim the beans (snap off one end and pull the stringy part off). Cook with a small amount of vegetable oil in a sauté pan over medium-high heat for 2–3 minutes. Sprinkle with salt or lemon juice. One pound will serve 4 people.

Turkey Paillards with Balsamic Sauce

Paillards are the same as cutlets: thin slices of meat that can be sautéed, grilled, or fried. They are a real friend on a busy day because they cook in a matter of minutes.

8 large garlic cloves, peeled and left whole
2 tablespoons all-purpose flour
1½ pounds turkey cutlets
3–4 tablespoons extra virgin olive oil
2 tablespoons pareve margarine
Freshly ground black pepper, to taste
½ cup chicken stock
½ cup red wine
¼ cup balsamic vinegar

Preheat the oven to 200°F. Place the garlic cloves in a pan, cover them with water, and bring to a boil over high heat. Cook for 6 minutes, drain, and set aside; cut them in half if very large. Spread the flour in a plate, dredge the cutlets in the flour, and shake to remove the excess. Heat 2 tablespoons olive oil and 1 tablespoon margarine in a sauté pan over medium heat and cook the turkey a few pieces at a time for 2–3 minutes per side or until they are lightly browned and crispy. Add up to 1 more tablespoon olive oil, if necessary to prevent sticking. Season to taste with pepper, place the turkey on a serving plate, and keep warm in the oven. Pour the remaining olive oil into the pan and add the garlic cloves. Cook for 4–5 minutes or until they are lightly browned. Add the chicken stock, wine, and vinegar. Raise the heat and bring the liquid to a boil, stirring with a whisk. Cook for about 5 minutes or until the liquid has reduced by half. Stir in the remaining 1 tablespoon margarine and blend it in. Pour the sauce over the turkey and serve. Makes 4 servings.

CORNISH HEN AND DUCK

Grilled Turkish-Style Cornish Hens

Rock Cornish hens are elegant little birds. Cutting them down the back into a butterfly shape gives them an even more attractive look and cuts cooking time to less than a half-hour. The sweet, mild meat is a delicious foil for the sturdy seasonings in this recipe. I like to serve these hens with Garlic and Scallion Smashed Potatoes (page 182), Sautéed Carrots with Mint and Shallots (page 194), Stir-Fried Fennel (page 198), or Roasted Asparagus (page 190).

> 2 Cornish hens
> ⅓ cup extra virgin olive oil
> ¼ cup lemon juice
> 2 large garlic cloves, minced
> 2 teaspoons ground cumin
> ½ teaspoon ground turmeric
> ¼ teaspoon cayenne pepper
> ⅛ teaspoon ground cinnamon

Rinse and dry the hens and cut them lengthwise along the back (the hens will still be attached at the breast). Place the hens in a nonreactive dish. Combine the olive oil, lemon juice, garlic, cumin, turmeric, cayenne, and cinnamon in a small bowl. Whisk the ingredients until they are well blended. Pour the dressing over the hens and marinate for 30–60 minutes. Turn the hens once or twice during this time. Preheat an outdoor grill or oven broiler with the rack about 6 inches from the heat source. Remove the hens from the marinade and broil or grill for about 25 minutes, turning the pieces occasionally, or until cooked through. Makes 4 servings.

Pan-Roasted Duck Breast with Chinese Flavors

This is easy enough for a special family dinner, but lovely enough for company, too. Serve it with a side dish such as stir-fried broccoli or baby bok choy or as a warm salad: slice the meat and place it over greens, frisée, or cooked lentils. You can make the sauce a day ahead.

4 boneless duck breast halves, about 8 ounces each
1 tablespoon vegetable oil
1 teaspoon sesame oil
2 dried red chile peppers
3 medium scallions, minced
1 large garlic clove, minced
1½ teaspoons minced fresh ginger
1 teaspoon finely grated fresh orange peel
½ cup hoisin sauce
¼ cup rice wine vinegar
Vegetable oil
Salt, to taste

Preheat the oven to 350°F. Wipe the surface of the duck and score the skin, being careful not to cut into the flesh. Heat 1 teaspoon vegetable oil and the sesame oil in a small saucepan over medium heat. Add the chile peppers and cook for 1 minute. Add the scallions, garlic, ginger, and orange peel and cook for 2–3 minutes or until the vegetables have softened and the peppers are browned. Add the hoisin sauce and vinegar, lower the heat, and cook for 5–6 minutes. Set aside. Remove the peppers and discard them. Heat a sauté pan over medium-high heat and brush the bottom with the remaining 2 teaspoons vegetable oil. Sear the duck breasts skin side up for 2 minutes, turn skin side down, and cook for 4 minutes, or until the skin is golden brown and crispy. Drain the fat from the pan. Glaze the duck breasts with the sauce. Place the pan in the oven and roast skin side up for 7–8 minutes or until the breasts are cooked through. Remove from the oven and baste the breasts with the pan juices. Let rest for 5–6 minutes before slicing and serving. Makes 4 servings.

Two dried peppers will give you a moderately spiced dish; if you like it hotter, use 3 or 4 peppers.

EGGS AND DAIRY

One of the most significant tenets of kosher cooking comes from the biblical prohibition against "seething a calf in its mother's milk." For millennia, that phrase has been interpreted to mean that meat and dairy products must be separated; they cannot be cooked or eaten together.

Kosher cooks have made the most of this particular challenge. Dairy dishes have always been a vital part of kosher cooking, whether in traditional Jewish dishes such as blintzes and kugels or American-style foods such as macaroni and cheese or a chilled soup finished with yogurt.

Eggs are immeasurably important not just for kosher cooks but throughout the world, for all cultures and cuisines. They're a good source of high quality protein and are relatively inexpensive, filling but not high in calories. They are quick and easy to cook and they're versatile. You can scramble eggs, fry them, boil them, and bake them. Use them in an omelet or frittata. Blend them with milk into custard or quiche, French toast, or pancakes.

But for kosher cooks, eggs hold an indispensable, singular place of honor. In addition to their other merits, eggs are also pareve. They aren't meat or dairy, so you can use them no matter what kind of meal you prepare. What a blessing! You can add a hard-cooked egg to a steak salad or make such dishes as Turkey Meatball Soup with Egg and Spinach (page 39). You can eat a cheese omelet, steak and eggs, or a chicken sausage frittata.

In the kosher kitchen, each egg must be inspected before you use it for cooking. The rules of kashruth state that a blood spot is a sign that the egg may have been fertilized; both the blood and the remainder of the egg must be discarded.

Egg and dairy dishes are often regarded as the stuff of breakfast or brunch. But there's no reason to limit them to morning fare: Challah French Toast with Cranberry-Orange Sauce (page 157), Lemon Cottage Cheese Pancakes (page 151), and Scrambled Eggs with Tomatoes and Feta Cheese (page 161) can be welcome as a light dinner, and substantial preparations such as Huevos Rancheros (page 152) or Peppers and Eggs (Shakshouka) (page 158) are filling and satisfying enough for an evening meal. None of these dishes takes too long to prepare, so they're naturals for busy weekday dinners, too.

Kosher Quick Guide

EGGS AND DAIRY

✓ Meat and dairy may not be eaten together.
✓ Eggs that have blood spots must be discarded.

Broiled Eggplant Parmesan

Eggplant Parmesan can be heavy and fattening. I prefer it unbreaded and broiled, so it's a lot lighter and less caloric, yet filling enough for dinner. I make this with plum tomatoes because they aren't as watery as regular tomatoes, which means the sauce will be thicker.

1 large eggplant, about 1½ pounds
6–7 tablespoons extra virgin olive oil
I onion, chopped
2 large garlic cloves, minced
10 large plum tomatoes, coarsely chopped
2 tablespoons minced fresh basil
Freshly ground black pepper, to taste
8 ounces shredded mozzarella cheese (about 2 cups)
3 tablespoons freshly grated Parmesan cheese

Preheat the oven broiler. Cut the eggplant lengthwise into thin slices (about ¼ inch). Using 4 5 tablespoons olive oil, lightly brush both sides of each eggplant slice. Place the slices on cookie sheets and broil for 6–8 minutes or until softened and lightly browned. Remove from the broiler and turn the oven to bake at 350°F. While the eggplant is broiling, heat the remaining 2 tablespoons olive oil in a sauté pan over medium heat. Add the onion and cook for 3 minutes, stirring occasionally, or until softened. Add the garlic and cook briefly. Add the tomatoes, basil, and pepper to taste and cook, stirring occasionally, for 12–15 minutes or until the tomatoes are very soft and most of the liquid has evaporated from the pan. Place one layer of eggplant in a lightly oiled baking dish and top with half the tomatoes. Repeat the eggplant-tomato layer. Sprinkle the mozzarella cheese on top. Sprinkle with Parmesan cheese. Bake for 10–15 minutes or until the cheese has melted and is bubbly. Makes 4 servings.

Do yourself a favor and buy a garlic press. Although some cooks say pressed garlic doesn't have the finesse of the chopped kind, for casseroles like this one and for sauces and marinades, it will be just fine.

Cheese and Corn Arepas with Eggs

Arepas are cornmeal pancakes that are popular in South America and have made inroads here in the United States as a snack or breakfast food. They can be fried, baked, or grilled. Sometimes arepas are cut in half and filled like a sandwich, sometimes they're served with cheese or meat. These Cheese and Corn Arepas are perfect when you're yearning for breakfast foods at dinner. Round out the meal by serving them with eggs and Tomato-Avocado Salad (page 63). Arepa flour is not difficult to find. Many traditional supermarkets carry it, typically in an ethnic foods aisle with other Latin ingredients.

Arepas

1 cup milk
4 tablespoons butter
1½ cups arepa flour
2 teaspoons sugar
1 teaspoon salt
2 tablespoons minced fresh jalapeño pepper
1 cup grated cheddar cheese
1 cup thawed frozen corn kernels
2 tablespoons vegetable oil

Heat 1¾ cups water, milk, and butter together until they are hot and the butter has melted. Set aside. Place the arepa flour, sugar, salt, jalapeño pepper, cheese, and corn kernels in a bowl. Pour in the liquid and stir to combine ingredients thoroughly. Let stand until all the liquid has been absorbed. Heat some of the oil in a sauté pan, preferably nonstick, over medium heat. Form the arepa dough into eight to twelve pancakes about ¼ inch thick. Cook the arepas for 6–8 minutes per side or until crispy, using more oil as necessary to prevent sticking. Serve with Sunnyside Eggs. Makes 4 servings.

Sunnyside Eggs

8 large eggs
1 tablespoon butter

Crack each egg into a small bowl, then carefully transfer it to a larger bowl. Set aside. Heat the butter in a large sauté pan over medium heat. When the butter has melted and looks foamy, pour the eggs into the pan. Cook them for about 3–4 minutes, piercing bubbles that appear in the whites, until the whites have set and are cooked to the degree of doneness desired. Makes 4 servings.

Lemon Cottage Cheese Pancakes

This recipe for delicate, fluffy pancakes is a superb choice for a weekday dinner when you yearn for something light. The lemon adds a refreshing quality, too. The dish is also nice for a relaxing weekend breakfast. I've made the pancakes for weekend guests and followed with Grapefruit and Orange Salad (page 64) to make the meal more festive.

1⅓ cups dry curd cottage cheese, pot cheese,
   or farmer cheese
3 large eggs
1 cup milk
1½ tablespoons finely grated fresh lemon peel
1 cup all-purpose flour
2 tablespoons sugar
1 teaspoon baking powder
½ teaspoon salt
Butter for the griddle

Combine the cottage cheese, eggs, milk, and lemon peel in a bowl. Add the flour, sugar, baking powder, and salt and mix to combine ingredients. Heat a griddle over medium heat and add a small amount of butter. When the butter has melted and looks foamy, working in batches, pour about ¼ cup batter onto the griddle for each pancake. Cook the pancakes for about 2 minutes per side, or until they are golden brown, adding more butter to the pan as necessary. Makes 4 servings.

Huevos Rancheros

This Mexican dish means "Ranch-Style Eggs." It's attractive, so you can serve it to company. Make the salsa ahead—even a day or two—to save time (store it in a covered container in the refrigerator). The salsa is medium hot—add more jalapeño if you prefer spicier food, or switch to a hotter pepper like habanero or serrano.

> 2 tablespoons extra virgin olive oil
> 1 large onion, chopped
> 3 tablespoons minced fresh jalapeño pepper
> 2 large garlic cloves, minced
> 3 large tomatoes, chopped
> 2 teaspoons minced fresh cilantro
> ½ teaspoon salt, or to taste
> Freshly ground black pepper, to taste
> 8 corn tortillas, wrapped in aluminum foil
> 1 tablespoon butter
> 8 large eggs
> 1½ cups shredded Monterey Jack cheese

Preheat the oven broiler with the rack about 6 inches from the heat source. Heat the olive oil in a sauté pan over medium heat. Add the onion and jalapeño pepper and cook for 2–3 minutes, stirring occasionally, or until the vegetables have softened. Add the garlic and cook briefly. Add the tomatoes, cilantro, salt, and pepper. Turn the heat to low and simmer, stirring occasionally, for about 15 minutes or until the ingredients are soft and most of the pan liquid has evaporated. Remove the pan from heat but cover the ingredients to keep them warm. Place the wrapped tortillas in the oven on the lowest shelf. While the sauce is cooking, heat the butter in a sauté pan over medium heat. When the butter has melted and looks foamy, crack the eggs into a small bowl one at a time, then transfer into the pan and cook for 2–3 minutes, piercing bubbles that appear in the whites until the whites have almost set and the eggs are nearly done. Unwrap the tortillas and place them in a baking dish, overlapping each other, to cover the bottom and lower sides of the dish. Place the eggs over the tortillas. Spoon the vegetable mixture over eggs. Sprinkle with the cheese. Broil for 3–4 minutes or until the ingredients are heated and the cheese has melted. Makes 4 servings.

Grape Tomato, Cheese, and Herb Omelet

Omelets are amazingly forgiving and this one is no exception. You can use dry cottage cheese, pot cheese, feta, cheddar, or mozzarella instead of the Swiss, and regular, chopped tomatoes for the grape tomatoes. Add chopped scallions if you like. Omelets are always wonderful when you serve them with crusty bread.

> 4–5 large eggs, beaten
> 2 tablespoons milk or water
> Salt and freshly ground black pepper, to taste
> 2 tablespoons minced mixed fresh herbs such as chives,
>   parsley, and thyme
> 2 tablespoons butter
> ⅓ cup halved grape tomatoes
> ¼ cup shredded Swiss cheese

Beat the eggs with the milk, salt, pepper, and herbs. Melt the butter in an omelet pan or other skillet with rounded sides over medium heat. When the butter has melted and looks foamy, add the eggs. As the edges of the eggs begin to set, use a rigid spatula to push the edges toward the center of the pan while tilting the pan to let uncooked portions move to the exposed surfaces. Keep pushing the eggs and tilting the pan until the eggs are almost set but still creamy and shiny. Spoon the tomatoes and cheese on top of the eggs, down the center. Fold the omelet in half or in thirds. Slide out onto a serving plate. Makes 2 servings.

Omelet pans were once mysterious things—food professionals said that the pans had to be seasoned, wiped out but left unwashed, and used only for omelets. The truth is you can make an omelet in any slope-sided pan. Nonstick pans are especially handy because the eggs slide out so easily, even with little fat used. For the best results, use a heavy, deep pan so that the eggs can cook on the bottom and stay moist on top.

Frittata with Winter Greens and Two Cheeses

This frittata begins with basic braised winter greens, which you can prepare separately as a side dish for a meat meal or with other vegetarian entrées. When I'm not in the mood for strong-tasting greens, I make this dish using spinach or chard.

1 bunch winter greens (mustard, kale, or collards)
2 tablespoons extra virgin olive oil
1 garlic clove, minced, optional
2 tablespoons water or vegetable stock
8 large eggs, beaten
2 tablespoons milk
1 tablespoon minced fresh parsley
2 tablespoons butter
1 medium onion, chopped
1 cup ricotta cheese
½ cup shredded mozzarella cheese
Salt and freshly ground black pepper, to taste

Preheat the oven broiler with the rack about 6 inches from the heat source. Wash the greens thoroughly, discard any thick, heavy stems, and let them air dry or dry them on a towel or in a salad spinner. Chop or tear them coarsely. Heat the olive oil in a sauté pan over medium heat. Add the garlic, if using, and cook for about 1 minute, to brown lightly. Add the greens and cook for 2–3 minutes or until the vegetables wilt slightly. Pour in the water or stock and cook, covered, stirring occasionally, for 5 minutes. Transfer the greens to a dish and wipe out the pan. Mix the eggs, milk, and parsley, and set aside. Heat the butter in the sauté pan over medium heat.

You can bake the frittata instead of broiling it. Preheat the oven to 375°F. After the frittata bottom has set on the stove top, bake the frittata for about 12–15 minutes, until the eggs are set and are puffed and golden brown.

Cut the frittata into small pieces to serve as hors d'oeuvres.

When the butter has melted and looks foamy, add the onion and cook for 4–5 minutes, stirring occasionally, or until the onions are soft and beginning to brown. Stir in the greens. Add the ricotta cheese by spooning small clumps on top of the vegetables. Pour in the egg mixture and turn the heat to low. Scatter the mozzarella cheese on top. Stir once or twice, then cook undisturbed for 8–10 minutes, or until the bottom has set. Place the pan under the broiler until the frittata is puffed and golden, about 1–2 minutes. Season to taste with salt and pepper. Makes 4 servings.

Edamame Succotash and Feta Cheese Quiche

Quiche is easy if you use a store-bought crust, and makes for a light but filling dinner. I've made this quiche with peas or lima beans instead of the edamame and used goat cheese instead of feta. If you like sweet red bell peppers, you can include 2–3 chopped tablespoonfuls to the other ingredients.

1 (9-inch) pie crust
1 small onion, chopped
½ cup fresh or thawed frozen edamame
½ cup fresh or thawed frozen corn kernels
¾ cup crumbled feta cheese
2 tablespoons minced fresh parsley
3 large eggs
⅔ cup half-and-half cream
⅔ cup whole milk
½ teaspoon salt, or to taste
Freshly ground black pepper, to taste

Preheat the oven to 400°F. Place aluminum foil over the pie crust and weight the foil down with beans or baking pellets. Bake for 10 minutes. Remove the foil and weights. Return the crust to the oven and bake for 3 minutes. Remove from the oven and lower the oven heat to 375°F. Place the onion, edamame, corn, feta cheese, and parsley on the bottom of the partially baked crust. Beat the eggs, cream, milk, salt, and pepper together until well blended and pour over the contents in the crust. Bake for about 40 minutes or until golden brown and set. Makes 4 servings.

Pie Crust

1½ cups all-purpose flour

¼ teaspoon salt

4 tablespoons butter

3 tablespoons vegetable shortening

3 tablespoons milk or cold water

Mix the flour and salt in a bowl. Add the butter and shortening in chunks and work the fats into the dry ingredients with your fingers or a pastry blender. Add the milk and form the ingredients into a soft ball of dough. Knead once or twice to blend ingredients thoroughly. Roll out the dough on a lightly floured surface and fit it into a 9- or 10-inch tart pan with removable sides. Makes enough for one tart crust (will also fit a standard 9-inch pie pan).

If you make your own pie crust, fit it into a tart pan with removable sides. This dough will be enough for a 9- or 10-inch pan. It may sound funny, but some 9-inch store-bought pie crusts are deeper than others yet they are not as deep as homemade pie crusts made in standard-size pie pans. If you use a deep-dish store-bought crust or one that's homemade, you'll have to bake the pie longer and increase the liquid ingredients in the quiche to ¾ cup for both cream and milk, and add one more egg.

To be sure the crust is tender, let dough rest for at least 30 minutes after you prepare it and before you roll it out.

Challah French Toast
with Cranberry-Orange Sauce

There's no better French toast than the kind you make with luxuriously rich, eggy challah. For a change, try this citrusy version with cranberry sauce instead of the usual maple syrup. The cranberry sauce can double as a side dish for your Thanksgiving turkey.

6 large eggs
½ cup whole milk
½ teaspoon vanilla extract
1 teaspoon finely grated fresh orange peel
8 slices challah or brioche, cut 1 inch thick
1½ tablespoons unsalted butter

Preheat the oven to 140°F. Beat the eggs, milk, vanilla extract, and orange peel in a large shallow pan. Add the bread slices and let them soak, turning them occasionally, until all of the liquid has been absorbed. Heat 1½ tablespoons butter in a large sauté pan over medium heat. When the butter has melted and looks foamy, add the soaked bread and cook for about 2 minutes per side or until lightly browned and crispy. Place the slices on a cookie sheet and keep them warm in the oven; repeat with remaining bread, adding more butter if needed. Serve with maple syrup or Cranberry-Orange Sauce. Makes 4 servings.

Cranberry-Orange Sauce

2 cups fresh cranberries
½ cup sugar
¼ cup orange juice
¼ cup sweet orange marmalade, optional

Combine the berries, sugar, and orange juice in a saucepan. Bring to a boil over high heat, lower the heat to medium, and cook for about 10 minutes or until the berries have popped and the mixture is saucelike. Remove the pan from the heat. Mix in the marmalade and let cool. Makes about 1½ cups.

Peppers and Eggs

This is a really easy version of shakshouka, a traditional Israeli tomato and egg dish. The sauce is spicy, a perfect foil for the rich, runny egg yolks. Shakshouka is a breakfast dish, a lunch dish, or it's for dinner (I like to serve Peppers and Eggs with warm pita and a salad if they're for dinner). Make extra "sauce" and heat it up to serve over bread for a yummy snack.

¼ cup extra virgin olive oil
1 medium onion, chopped
1 red bell pepper, deseeded and chopped
2 small habanero or red chile peppers, deseeded
    and minced
1 large garlic clove, minced
6–8 plum tomatoes, coarsely chopped
1 tablespoon minced fresh basil
1 tablespoon lemon juice
8 large eggs
¾ teaspoon zatar

Heat the olive oil in a large sauté pan over medium heat. Add the onion, bell pepper, and habanero peppers. Cook for 4–5 minutes or until softened slightly. Add the garlic and cook briefly. Add the tomatoes, basil, and lemon juice, stir, cover the pan, turn the heat to low, and cook for 8–10 minutes, stirring occasionally, or until vegetables are very soft and saucelike. Crack the eggs into a small bowl one at a time, then transfer each one next to another over the vegetables. Cover the pan and cook for 4–5 minutes or until the eggs are set but yolks are still slightly runny. Sprinkle with zatar. Serve each person two eggs and some of the vegetables. Makes 4 servings.

Cracking the eggs one at a time into a small cup before adding them to any dish lets you inspect each egg for blood spots or spoilage.

Be careful when working with chile peppers. The burning sensation that we find so pleasurable to the palate can sting your skin. Try to work with thin disposable gloves but if you don't, after you've handled the peppers, wash your hands several times before inserting contact lenses or touching your mouth, face, or any part of your body that might have a cut or open wound.

Potato and Charred Poblano Tortilla

A tortilla is a flat Spanish omelet, similar to a frittata. It's a terrific brunch dish but also fine for dinner. I've also used this tortilla (and others) for hors d'oeuvres: cut the omelet into small squares. Tortillas don't have to be piping hot. They're just as good at room temperature, so don't worry about timing. Tomato salad would make a good side dish.

>2 large russet-type (baking) potatoes
>¼ cup extra virgin olive oil
>1 large onion, chopped
>1 large poblano pepper, deseeded and minced
>¼ cup minced fresh cilantro, optional
>8 large or extra-large eggs, beaten
>¾ cup crumbled feta cheese (or grated cheddar)
>Salt and freshly ground black pepper, to taste

Preheat the oven broiler with the rack about 6 inches from the heat source. Peel the potatoes and cut them into ½-inch pieces. Heat the olive oil in a large nonstick sauté pan over medium heat. Add the potatoes and cook them, covered, for 5 minutes, stirring 2–3 times. Add the onion, poblano pepper, and optional cilantro and continue to cook, stirring occasionally, uncovered, for 3–4 minutes. Add the eggs and cheese and cook without stirring for 2 minutes, then gently move the edges toward the center to allow liquid egg to spill over the side and onto the bottom of the pan. Cook for another minute or until the eggs are almost set and the bottom is golden brown. Place the pan in the broiler and cook briefly to brown the top. Invert onto a platter to serve. Sprinkle with salt and pepper to taste. Cut into wedges. Makes 4 servings.

A poblano is a fairly mild pepper. You can substitute an Anaheim for this recipe, but if you like a tortilla that's hot and spicy, switch to one of the more fiery varieties: jalapeño, serrano, habanero, or Scotch bonnets.

Roasted Vegetable Pizza

I always keep a ball of pizza dough in the freezer in case I feel like making pizza. Thaw the dough in the refrigerator overnight and it's ready the next day. You can also make this with a pre-baked crust. Pizza is always a good bet for dinner because it's well liked by so many people. This one is more like an extra-large, open-face sandwich than a pizza. It's loaded with vegetables, so this can be classified as "healthy pizza"!

1 medium portobello mushroom cap, cut into
¾-inch chunks
½ medium eggplant, about 8 ounces, cut into
¾-inch chunks
5 tablespoons extra virgin olive oil
Salt, to taste
1 pound pizza dough
1 small red onion, sliced
3 plum tomatoes, sliced ¼ inch thick
½ red bell pepper, cut into 1-inch chunks
6 medium asparagus spears, cut into 2-inch pieces
6–8 arugula leaves, torn
2 cups shredded mozzarella cheese (about 8 ounces)
2 tablespoons freshly grated Parmesan cheese

Preheat oven to 450°F. If you have a pizza stone, be sure to place it in the oven and preheat it as well. Place one rack in top third of oven, the other rack in the bottom third. Combine the mushroom and eggplant and toss with 2 tablespoons of the olive oil. Place on a cookie sheet, sprinkle with salt and roast on the top shelf for 10 minutes, turning once or twice. While the vegetables roast, stretch the pizza dough into a 12- to 15-inch circle and place on a pizza peel or lightly oiled pizza pan or cookie sheet. Prick the dough with the tines of a fork. Brush with 1 tablespoon olive oil. Set aside. Add the red onion, tomatoes, red pepper, and asparagus to the vegetables, pour in remaining olive oil and toss ingredients. Return the vegetables to the oven. At the same time, slide the pizza dough onto the pizza stone (or place the pizza pan or cookie sheet on the bottom rack). Bake for 12 minutes. Remove the pizza and vegetables. Place the hot vegetables onto the partially baked crust. Top with the mozzarella cheese. Scatter the arugula leaves on top. Sprinkle with Parmesan cheese. Bake for another 4–5 minutes or until the cheese is hot and bubbly. Makes 4 servings.

A pizza stone is a handy tool if you bake pizza with any regularity. It's a large tile that retains heat and keeps the cooking temperature even so pizza crusts will always be crispy. A peel helps you slide the pie onto and off the stone.

Scrambled Eggs
with Tomatoes and Feta Cheese

This dish is an Americanized and easy version of Turkish menemen, an egg and tomato dish that is equally wonderful for breakfast, brunch, or dinner. It's an accommodating dish that usually includes onions, bell peppers, and parsley, but you can also add cheese, as I've done here. I also prefer sharper, more refreshing scallions to the classic yellow onions.

> 2 tablespoons butter, extra virgin olive oil,
>   or a combination of the two
> 4 medium scallions, chopped
> 1 medium red bell pepper, deseeded and chopped
> 3 medium tomatoes, chopped
> 8 large eggs, beaten
> 6 ounces crumbled feta cheese
> 2–3 tablespoons minced fresh flat-leaf parsley
> Salt and freshly ground black pepper, to taste

Heat the butter or olive oil in a sauté pan over medium heat. When the butter has melted and looks foamy, add the scallions and bell pepper and cook for a minute or two. Add the tomatoes and cook for about 3–4 minutes or until they have softened. Add the eggs and feta cheese and cook, stirring frequently, until eggs are cooked through but still creamy. Sprinkle with parsley and season to taste with salt and pepper. Makes 4 servings.

Spinach Pie

This is such a family favorite that I always have one of these pies in my freezer. Although most recipes for this classic dish call for chopped spinach, I prefer the whole leaf because it has a superior texture and I think the quality of the spinach is better.

2 (10-ounce) packages frozen spinach, thawed
2 tablespoons extra virgin olive oil
1 medium onion, chopped
3 large eggs
8 ounces feta cheese, crumbled
6 tablespoons freshly grated Parmesan cheese
1 tablespoon minced fresh dill
Freshly ground black pepper, to taste
4 sheets phyllo dough
2 tablespoons butter, melted

Preheat the oven to 400°F. Squeeze as much water out of the spinach as possible and set aside. Heat the olive oil in a sauté pan over medium heat, add the onion, and cook for 2–3 minutes or until softened. Stir in the spinach and mix well. Remove the pan from the heat and add the eggs, feta cheese, Parmesan cheese, dill, and pepper to taste. Place in an 8- or 9-inch square cake pan or a rectangular baking dish. Place one phyllo sheet on top of the spinach mixture (tuck edges under if needed). Brush with some of the melted butter. Repeat with remaining phyllo and butter. Bake for about 20 minutes or until golden brown. Makes 4 servings.

For a change, use thawed frozen puff pastry (trim the dough to fit the top of the baking pan). Brush the pastry with an egg wash (one egg with 2 teaspoons water) rather than the melted butter.

Tzadziki

Tzadziki is a wonder. It's a side dish with salads or egg dishes. It's a terrific dip with crudités, chips, or crackers. And it's a flavorful, tangy sauce that brightens the taste of grilled vegetable pitas. Think about tzadziki when you're having company or when you're looking for a healthy snack.

> 3 cups plain yogurt (nonfat is fine)
> 3 medium cucumbers
> 1 large garlic clove, minced
> 3 tablespoons minced fresh mint
> 2 tablespoons minced fresh dill
> 1 teaspoon kosher salt
> 3 tablespoons lemon juice
> 1 tablespoon extra virgin olive oil

Place a double layer of cheesecloth in a strainer. Spoon the yogurt into the lined strainer and set it over a bowl. Refrigerate for 4 hours. Place the yogurt in a bowl; discard the fluids that have collected in the bowl. Peel the cucumbers and cut them in half lengthwise. Scoop out and discard the seeds. Grate the cucumber in a food processor or by hand. Strain the cucumber in a sieve, pressing down to extract as much liquid as possible, then discard the liquid. When the yogurt is ready, stir in the cucumbers, garlic, mint, dill, salt, lemon juice, and olive oil. Stir to blend all the ingredients thoroughly. Makes about 4 cups.

White Pizza with Spinach

This pizza can be even easier to prepare if you use a pre-baked pizza crust.

> 1 pound pizza dough
> 3 tablespoons extra virgin olive oil
> 1 large garlic clove, minced
> 1 bunch fresh spinach, washed and dried
> 1 (15-ounce) container ricotta cheese
> 8 ounces shredded mozzarella, about 2 cups
> 1½ tablespoons freshly grated Parmesan cheese
> 1 teaspoon dried oregano

Preheat the oven to 450°F. If you have a pizza stone, be sure to place it in the oven and preheat it as well. Stretch the pizza dough into a 12- to 15-inch circle and place on a pizza peel or lightly oiled pizza pan or cookie sheet. Heat 2 tablespoons olive oil in a sauté pan over medium heat. Add the garlic and cook briefly. Add the spinach and cook for 3–5 minutes or until wilted and all the liquid has evaporated from the pan. If necessary, press the spinach in a sieve to extract liquid. Chop the spinach coarsely. Spread the ricotta cheese evenly over the pizza dough. Top with the spinach. Spread the mozzarella cheese on top. Sprinkle with Parmesan cheese and oregano. Drizzle with remaining tablespoon olive oil. Slide the pizza dough onto the pizza stone (or place the pizza pan or cookie sheet on the bottom rack of the oven). Bake the pizza for 15–18 minutes, or until the crust is crispy and the cheese has melted and is golden brown. Makes 4 servings.

SANDWICHES

What do you eat when you're on the run? A sandwich is always a good choice. After all, it was invented by a man who had no time to waste. Some say that John Montagu, the Fourth Earl of Sandwich, was an inveterate gambler and he didn't want to leave the gaming tables, so he had his chef stuff dinner between two slices of bread.

We've come a long way since Montagu's eighteenth-century creation. Today the sandwich category includes wraps, filled pitas, panini, triple-layer clubs, and open-face versions with only one slice of bread.

What makes a perfect sandwich? Is it the filling? The bread? The spread?

The answer is: all of the above. I know a man who once ordered a roast beef sandwich with Russian dressing on pumpernickel, but when he was told that pumpernickel wasn't available, he switched his entire order to a grilled steak sandwich with tomatoes and olive oil on a crusty roll.

Most of us are not that fussy. After all, a good sandwich is often a spontaneous bit of this and that—on bread. But it's still like any other recipe. It may be accommodating, but all the elements have to work together. When you make a sandwich, you have to consider taste and texture. The reason that panini are so popular is that the crunch of bread and the ooze of whatever's inside (usually cheese) make a perfect textural balance, like yin and yang in a sandwich. The Sort of Cubano (page 177) is that sort of dish, a kosher take on the traditional version.

Most of the time, a sandwich won't be enough for dinner. But hamburgers surely are. When you're looking for a burger that's a bit different, try the Lamburgers with Sun-Dried Tomato Mayo (page 174), or the Salmon Burgers with Lemon-Chive Mayo (page 176). Three other recipes—grilled or sautéed Marinated Skirt Steak Sandwich with Herbal Mayonnaise (page 171), Tuna Melts (page 178), and Jalapeño Monterey Jack–Chipotle Grilled Wrap (page 173) are also substantial and will fill you up.

On the other hand, if you're craving just a light bite to eat, try the Grilled Cheese and Pear Sandwich (page 170) or Grilled Eggplant, Tomato, and Feta Cheese Sandwich (page 169).

Crisped Gilboa Cheese Panini
with Fig Jam

This recipe is an updated and sophisticated take on old-fashioned grilled cheese. Gilboa, a kosher cheese named for the Gilboa Mountains in Israel, is a delightful, hard, tangy, sheep's milk cheese similar to manchego. It's useful for sandwiches and also on a cheese board, accompanied by fig jam. Many supermarkets carry it (some separate the kosher cheeses in a special refrigerated section).

> 1 ciabatta or other crusty roll
> 1 tablespoon cream cheese
> 1½ tablespoons fig jam (apricot jam is fine, too)
> 1 ounce Gilboa (manchego) cheese, sliced

Slice the ciabatta roll in half. Spread the bottom with the cream cheese. Spread the fig jam on top. Top with the Gilboa slices. Cover with the top half of the roll. Heat a nonstick sauté pan or a cast-iron skillet over medium heat. Brush the surface with a small amount of butter or vegetable oil. Place the sandwich in the pan and place another pan on top. Weight the pan with canned goods. Cook for 2–3 minutes per side or until the outside is crispy and the cheese has melted. Makes one sandwich.

A panini grill makes sandwiches look terrific and professional, but the sandwich tastes just as good whatever equipment you use. Weighting down the bread helps keep the surface crispy, a great contrast to the soft melting cheese inside.

Egg and Chicken Sandwich
with Charmoula Mayonnaise

This sandwich will take you just a few minutes to put together—it's plain egg and chicken. What makes this sandwich different, livelier, tastier is the charmoula. To make this spicy, garlicky Moroccan-style condiment, see the recipe for Lamb Chops with Charmoula Pesto (page 107).

½ cup mayonnaise
3–4 teaspoons charmoula
8 slices multigrain bread
4 ounces sliced chicken
4 hard-cooked eggs, sliced
2 tomatoes, sliced

Mix the mayonnaise and charmoula together. Spread equal amounts on one side of each slice of bread. Place the chicken slices on each of four bread slices. Top with egg and tomato slices. Cover with second piece of bread. Makes four sandwiches.

I frequently have hard-cooked eggs on hand to use as a snack or for egg salad or sandwiches. They last about a week in the refrigerator. Many people call them hard-boiled eggs, but that's a misnomer. Eggs should never be boiled or they might become hard and rubbery. Hard-cooked eggs should be poached—cooked at a simmer. Here's the recipe: Place eggs in a large saucepan in a single layer if possible and cover with water. Bring the water to a boil. Immediately turn the heat down to keep the water at a simmer. Do not let the water boil again. Simmer for 10 minutes. Remove the pan from the heat, drain the eggs immediately under cold water. Peel when cool enough to handle (or leave unpeeled to use at a later time).

Grilled Eggplant, Tomato, and Feta Cheese Sandwich

This sandwich is so "meaty" and satisfying it's hard to believe it only contains vegetables and cheese. Our family loves this when we want something light for dinner. Occasionally, I will grill portobello mushroom caps and stuff them inside the sandwich as well.

> 6 tablespoons mayonnaise
> 1 large garlic clove, minced
> 1 tablespoon lemon juice
> Freshly ground black pepper, to taste
> 1 medium eggplant
> ⅓ cup extra virgin olive oil
> 1 large Vidalia onion
> 1 loaf French bread, 10 ounces
> 2 medium tomatoes, sliced
> 3 ounces crumbled feta cheese
> 3 tablespoons minced fresh mint
> 2 tablespoons minced fresh parsley

Preheat the oven broiler or outdoor grill with the rack about 4 inches from the heat source. Mix the mayonnaise, garlic, lemon juice, and pepper to taste and set aside. Cut the eggplant into ⅜-inch-thick slices and brush the slices with some of the olive oil. Cut the onion into ¼-inch-thick slices and brush them with the remaining olive oil. Broil or grill the vegetables for about 5–8 minutes, turning them once, or until they are tender. Remove and set aside. Cut the bread into four equal sections and slice each section in half lengthwise. Toast the bread cut side up in the broiler (or cut side down on the grill) for 45 seconds, or until lightly crispy. Spread the bottom bread halves with the mayonnaise mixture. Top with the eggplant, onion, and tomato slices. Place the cheese on top. Scatter with mint and parsley and cover with bread tops. Makes 4 sandwiches.

Eggplant can sometimes be bitter. **Some people salt the slices (use kosher salt) and let them "sweat" for 30–60 minutes. The beads of moisture that form on top of the slices should be wiped off with a paper towel. Salting not only removes bitterness but makes the eggplant very tender. In my experience, though, I often skip it—it is important only if you will be eating the eggplant by itself, not mixed with other flavorful ingredients that will balance out any bitterness.**

Grilled Cheese and Pear Sandwich

For grilled cheese lovers, here's another easy recipe. The texture of ripe, juicy pear is a terrific partner for any of the cheeses recommended; the fruit's sweet edge is a nice contrast to the sharpness of the cheese and the sweet spices and cayenne pepper play off each other as well. You can make the sandwich on any kind of bread but multigrain's nutty flavor and uneven texture make it the most interesting.

4 tablespoons softened butter
4 slices multigrain bread
4 ounces Muenster, Swiss, Fontina Fontal or cheddar
    cheese
1 ripe pear, peeled and cored
⅛ teaspoon each of: freshly grated nutmeg, ground
    cinnamon, ground ginger, and cayenne pepper

Butter both sides of each slice of multigrain bread. Cover two of the slices with equal amounts of cheese. Slice the pear and place on top of the cheese. Sprinkle each open sandwich with a pinch of nutmeg, cinnamon, ginger, and cayenne pepper. Place the second buttered slice of bread on top. Heat a sauté pan over medium heat and add the sandwiches. Fry for 2–3 minutes per side or until golden brown. Makes 2 sandwiches.

The sandwich is even better if you weight it down as it cooks (see the instructions for Crisped Gilboa Cheese Panini with Fig Jam, page 167).

Fontina Fontal is a mild kosher cheese available in the kosher cheese section of supermarkets. It tastes like a combination of Fontina and Swiss.

Marinated Skirt Steak Sandwich with Herbal Mayonnaise

I love skirt steak because it's so juicy. I make this sandwich on the grill in the summer and in the broiler in the winter, although if I haven't remembered to preheat the broiler I use a grill pan. I prefer the bread lightly toasted but, if I'm in one of my low-carb phases, I make this dish without the bread and serve the meat with the tomatoes and mayonnaise dressing. Whichever way you decide to serve it, you might want to include Grilled Balsamic Vinegar–Glazed Red Onions (page 184) and Pan-Fried Paprika Potatoes (page 192), or Garlic and Scallion Smashed Potatoes (page 182) on the side.

½ cup red wine vinegar
3 tablespoons red wine
2 tablespoons extra virgin olive oil
2 large garlic cloves, minced
2 teaspoons Dijon mustard
1½ pounds skirt steak
½ cup mayonnaise
2 tablespoons minced fresh basil
1 teaspoon minced fresh oregano (or ¼ teaspoon dried oregano)
4 club rolls or other crusty bread, plain or lightly toasted
2 tomatoes, sliced
Freshly ground black pepper, to taste

Combine the vinegar, red wine, olive oil, garlic, and 1 teaspoon mustard in a shallow nonreactive dish. Add the meat and turn it to coat both sides with the marinade. Let marinate for ½ to 2 hours. Preheat the oven broiler or outdoor grill with the rack about 4–6 inches from the heat source. Broil or grill the meat for about 3 minutes per side or until it has reached the degree of desired doneness. Remove from the heat and let rest on a cutting board. Combine the mayonnaise, remaining teaspoon mustard, and the basil and oregano. Spread equal quantities of the mayonnaise on the inside of each roll. Slice the meat and place equal quantities on each roll. Top with tomatoes and the second piece of bread. Sprinkle with pepper to taste. Makes 4 sandwiches.

Kosher skirt steak tends to be salty. If you have time, soak the meat in cold water for about 30 minutes before cooking.

Grilled Red Pepper, Portobello, and Cheese Sandwich

The contrast of cold cheese, hot, soft vegetables and crunchy bread makes this a sensation on the palate. It's a good choice for dinner on a summer day when you're in the mood for something light. But if you've got a yen for it in winter, cook the vegetables in the broiler. It's the kind of sandwich you can serve to TV watchers glued to the set for the Super Bowl or the Final Four.

> 1 large red bell pepper
> 4 medium or 2 large portobello mushroom caps
> ⅓ cup extra virgin olive oil
> 4 Portuguese rolls, sliced, or 8 slices round Italian bread
> ½ pound fresh mozzarella cheese, thinly sliced
> Salt and freshly ground black pepper, to taste
> ¼ cup minced fresh basil

Preheat the oven broiler or outdoor grill with the rack about 4 inches from the heat source. Remove the stem and seeds from the bell pepper and cut it into quarters. Clean the mushroom caps. Brush the pepper and mushroom caps with some of the olive oil. Grill the vegetables, turning them occasionally, for 8–10 minutes or until the pepper has charred and the mushrooms have softened. Transfer the vegetables to a plate. Place the rolls on the grill, cut-side down, for about 45 seconds to toast them lightly (or use a toaster oven). Cut the pepper quarters in half and lay two pieces on the bottoms of each of four rolls or slices of bread. Slice the mushrooms and place on top of the peppers. Place equal amounts of cheese on top. Drizzle with the remaining olive oil. Sprinkle with salt and pepper and the basil. Cover with remaining bread. Makes 4 sandwiches.

> If the vegetables are still hot the cheese will melt slightly. If not, put the sandwiches in the turned-off oven or grill for a minute or two.

Jalapeño Monterey Jack–Chipotle Grilled Wrap

This is another recipe given to me by my friends Judith Roll and Rebecca Martin, from the Sweet On You Bakery & Café at the JCC in Stamford, Connecticut. It's a large, filling sandwich that will satisfy the hungriest person in your house. I like it with more chipotle in adobo sauce, but if you prefer milder foods, either leave the chipotle out or just use a little of it.

> ½ cup mayonnaise
> 2 teaspoons minced chipotles in adobo
> 1 tablespoon freshly squeezed lime juice
> ¼ cup minced fresh cilantro
> Salt and freshly ground black pepper, to taste
> 4 (12-inch) flour tortillas
> 1 cup thinly-sliced mushrooms
> 1 pound sliced jalapeño Monterey Jack cheese
> 8 slices tomato
> 1 ripe Hass avocado, peeled, pitted, and sliced
> Vegetable oil

In a food processor, combine the mayonnaise, chipotle in adobo sauce, lime juice, cilantro, and salt and pepper to taste. Process until well blended. Spread equal amounts of the sauce on each tortilla. Lay the mushroom slices in a single layer on top of the sauce. Top with slices of cheese, tomato, and avocado. Fold the tortilla like a burrito (fold top and bottom over the ingredients, then fold both sides in to make a fully enclosed package). Heat a griddle, cast iron pan or nonstick pan over medium heat. Pour in a small amount of oil. Place the wraps in the pan and cook for about 2 minutes per side or until lightly browned and the cheese is melted. Makes 4 sandwiches.

Chipotles in adobo are smoked jalapeño peppers in a red sauce that contains tomato paste and spices. They are a fabulous flavor enhancer for lots of foods, not just sandwiches. You can add some to soups and stews, marinades, or rubs for grilled meats and poultry, or mix into mayonnaise.

Lamburgers
with Sun-Dried Tomato Mayo

How can you jazz up a plain old hamburger? Make it with ground lamb! These burgers are juicy and flavorful with fresh herbs and spices. Tangy sun-dried tomato mayonnaise replaces the traditional ketchup. If you prefer, you can cook these burgers on an outdoor grill or oven broiler rather than in a pan on the stove top.

20 ounces ground lamb
½ cup fresh bread crumbs
1 medium onion, chopped
1 large garlic clove, minced
1 large egg, beaten
¼ cup minced fresh parsley
2 tablespoons minced fresh mint
1½ teaspoons ground cumin
1 teaspoon paprika
⅛ teaspoon ground cinnamon
½ cup mayonnaise
¼ cup minced sun-dried tomatoes in oil, drained
1–2 tablespoons lemon juice
4 buns, rolls, or pita pockets, warmed

Combine the ground lamb, bread crumbs, onion, garlic, egg, parsley, mint, cumin, paprika, and cinnamon and mix to blend ingredients thoroughly. Shape the mixture into four burgers about 1 inch thick. Preheat a grill pan or sauté pan over high heat. Sear the burgers for 1 minute per side, then lower the heat to medium. Cook for another 2–3 minutes per side or until cooked through. While the burgers are cooking, mix together the mayonnaise, sun-dried tomatoes, and lemon juice. Place the cooked burgers on the bottom slice of bread and top each with a dollop of the mayonnaise. Cover with the remaining bread. Makes 4 sandwiches.

Red Pepper and Vidalia Onion Sandwich

This quick-fix sandwich is a good lunch item and is useful for dinner if you include a soup and salad. You can add on to the filling—leftover fish, capers, marinated artichoke hearts, and sun-dried tomatoes or fresh tomatoes all work.

2 medium red bell peppers
6 tablespoons extra virgin olive oil
2 medium Vidalia onions, thinly sliced
Salt and freshly ground black pepper, to taste
4 ciabatta or club rolls
8 slices provolone cheese

Remove the stem and seeds from the peppers and cut them into ¼-inch strips. Heat the olive oil in a sauté pan over medium heat. Add the peppers and the onions and cook for about 10 minutes, or until the vegetables are very soft and lightly golden. Sprinkle with salt and pepper. Cut the rolls in half and toast them. Place equal amounts of the filling on the bottoms. Scatter equal amounts of cheese on top and cover with the remaining bread. Makes 4 sandwiches.

Salmon Burgers with Lemon-Chive Mayo

Salmon burgers have really come into their own. Restaurants serve them and supermarkets sell them ready-to-cook. You can make them easily at home, too. The Lemon-Chive Mayo takes almost no time to mix, but you can substitute old-fashioned tartar sauce if you prefer.

1 pound skinless salmon fillet
2 scallions, minced
1 tablespoon fresh lemon juice
2 teaspoons Dijon mustard
2 teaspoons prepared white horseradish
½ cup fresh bread crumbs
Salt and freshly ground black pepper, to taste
1 tablespoon extra virgin olive oil
1 teaspoon butter
8 slices buttered white toast (use firm, home style bread)

Chop the salmon into tiny pieces and place in a bowl. Add the scallions, lemon juice, mustard, horseradish, bread crumbs, and salt and pepper to taste. (Alternatively, cut the fish into chunks and process the ingredients briefly in a food processor using on-off/pulse until the fish is chopped). Shape into four ¾- to 1-inch-thick patties. Heat the olive oil and butter in a sauté pan over high heat. When the butter has melted and looks foamy, turn the heat to medium and add the burgers. Cook for about 2–3 minutes per side, or until brown and crispy. Serve on buttered, toasted bread with equal amounts of Lemon-Chive Mayo. Makes 4 sandwiches.

Lemon-Chive Mayo

¼ cup mayonnaise
2 tablespoons minced fresh chives
1 teaspoon lemon juice
½ teaspoon Dijon mustard
¼ teaspoon finely grated fresh lemon peel

Mix the mayonnaise, chives, lemon juice, mustard, and lemon peel and set aside in the refrigerator. Makes about ½ cup.

Sort of Cubano

A classic Cubano sandwich is made with ham and roasted pork. This kosher version combines roasted turkey and corned beef in a tangy, tasty riff on the original. Vegetarian soy cheese looks and tastes just like the real thing, so nothing is missing from this sandwich. And you can jazz it up with chile peppers if you like it spicy.

4 crusty sandwich rolls or 8 pieces of home style
    white bread
¼ cup mayonnaise
2 tablespoons yellow mustard
2–3 teaspoons canned chipotles in adobo,
    minced, optional
¼ pound corned beef, thinly sliced
¼ pound roasted turkey, thinly sliced
6–8 Tofutti soy American-flavored slices
Several thin slices of dill pickle
Extra virgin olive oil, if needed

Slice the rolls in half. Spread equal amounts of the mayonnaise on one side of each roll, the mustard on the other side. Add the chipotles if using, placing them over the mayonnaise. Layer the meats on top of the mayonnaise. Cover with the soy American slices and pickle slices. Top with the mustard-covered bread half. Cook in a panini grill or sandwich grill if you have one. Or, heat a nonstick sauté pan over medium heat. Brush the surface with a small amount of olive oil. Arrange the sandwiches inside the pan and place another pan on top. Weight the pan with canned goods. Cook the sandwiches, turning once, for 5–6 minutes or until crispy on both sides. Makes 4 sandwiches.

Some soy cheeses are not dairy-free, so be sure to look at the label. Tofutti is pareve.

Tuna Melts

If you're a fan of tuna melts you'll love this version made with fresh fish. There's no mayo involved and it has a refreshing summer feel because of the basil and sliced tomato. But this sandwich is a good bet no matter what the weather. Serve it with a salad in summer—try Cucumber Salad (page 56) or Potato-Corn Salad with Basil Vinaigrette (page 62), a bowl of hot soup—consider Bean and Pasta Soup (page 30) or Tomato Soup with Chickpeas, Chard, and Harissa (page 33) when it's cold out.

> 1 pound fresh tuna, cut about 1¼ inches thick
> Salt and freshly ground black pepper, to taste
> 2 tablespoons extra virgin olive oil
> 4 slices round Italian bread
> 2 tablespoons minced fresh basil
> 1 large or 2 medium tomatoes, sliced
> ¾ cup grated Cheddar cheese

Preheat the oven broiler with the rack about 3–4 inches from the heat source. Sprinkle the fish with salt and pepper to taste. Heat the olive oil in a sauté pan over medium-high heat. Add the fish and cook for 2–3 minutes per side (if you prefer more well-done fish cook it 2–3 minutes longer) or until crispy on the outside. Transfer to a cutting board. Slice the fish and layer the pieces on the bread slices. Sprinkle the basil on top. Layer the tomato slices on top and cover with the cheese. Broil for about 2 minutes or until the cheese has melted and is bubbly. Makes 4 sandwiches.

VEGETABLES

Parents may still have trouble getting their kids to eat vegetables, but grown-ups have grown to love them. Farmers' markets are now favorite destination spots and even the bins at supermarkets entice with an abundance of gorgeous produce in a variety of shapes, sizes, and colors. Buying vegetables almost seems exciting.

Farmers' markets provide more than entertainment. They are among the prime places where you can buy local, in-season produce with a garden-fresh, just-picked flavor. And they help support local farmers and businesses. On the other hand, not everyone lives near a market that sells locally produced items. And some live in places where the growing season is a short few months in the summer, so local fruits and vegetables are unavailable for much of the year. Thanks to fast transport from warm, sunny places, we can get produce that's always in season—perhaps in California if not Connecticut—so there is almost no such thing as a "seasonal" vegetable anymore. We may not be able to find fresh peas or fiddleheads throughout the year, but there is a steady supply of familiar carrots, eggplant, spinach, and broccoli, and also lesser-known fennel, chard, and beet greens. You'll find purple and orange bell peppers, not just red and green, and all sorts of chile peppers too. Potatoes? There are russets and Yukon golds, new potatoes, purple potatoes, red bliss, and fingerlings. And several varieties of sweet potato. With all this bounty, you are sure to find a few vegetables that will please everyone in your family.

Vegetables are an important part of our diet. Everyone knows that they're healthy—studies show that eating vegetables may reduce the risk for stroke and other cardiovascular diseases as well as type-2 diabetes and some types of cancer. They also help keep your weight down—vegetables don't have a lot of calories so you can fill up without too much concern about putting on pounds.

For the home cook, vegetables add color, texture, and variety to a meal. Sweet Potato Pancakes (page 199) are golden-orange and crispy, Roasted Plum Tomatoes (page 191), richly red and tender. In this section you'll find a broad variety of vegetable recipes suitable for different kinds of meals and especially useful for kosher cooks. Most of the recipes are pareve or may become pareve by switching or leaving out an ingredient. The recipe for Eggplant with Yogurt and Pine Nuts (page 185) is filling enough to be a light lunch, but you can use it as part of a dairy or vegetarian meal—or eliminate the yogurt sauce and serve it with meat. Herb-Roasted Carrot and Parsnip "Fries" (page 187) are a lowfat alternative to the beloved french fries. Roasted Asparagus with Wasabi Mayonnaise (page 190) will work as an hors d'oeuvre, first course, or side dish.

When you're in a hurry to get dinner on the table, you might be tempted to steam vegetables and be done with it. Plain vegetables are always fine, but with a few minutes of prep work, say, chopping some fresh ginger or setting aside some pantry ingredients, you can serve dishes like Stir-Fried Broccoli with Orange Peel and Red Chile Peppers (page 197) or Crisped Cauliflower with Raisins and Pine Nuts (page 181). And look in the chapter on meats, where you'll find recipes for Beef Kebabs with Quick Pebre Sauce (page 103) and Lamb Chops with Charmoula Pesto (page 107). Both pebre (a Chilean condiment) and charmoula (a spicy Moroccan blend) add bountiful flavor to plain steamed vegetables, so I always save

2–3 teaspoons of the sauce when I make those recipes for those days when I have no time to fuss but want the vegetables to have some pizzazz. Smart but simple flavors and fixin's like these will make believers of even those last holdouts who may still think they don't like vegetables.

Crisped Cauliflower with Raisins and Pine Nuts

Cauliflower (the name means "cabbage flower") is an underused vegetable, perhaps because it turns to mush and has a strong odor when it's overcooked. But when it's properly prepared, cauliflower has a rich, nutty taste. Most people are familiar with the white variety, but the vegetable now comes in beautiful new fashion shades—orange and purple, for example. The color adds eye appeal to a dinner plate and the colored varieties are somewhat tamer, but they all taste much the same.

> 1 head cauliflower
> 4 tablespoons extra virgin olive oil
> ½ cup fresh bread crumbs
> 2 tablespoons pine nuts
> 1 large shallot, chopped
> 2 garlic cloves, minced
> ⅓ cup raisins
> 1 tablespoon lemon juice
> Salt and freshly ground black pepper, to taste

Cut the cauliflower into florets. Cook, covered, in lightly salted simmering water for 4–5 minutes or until just tender. Drain and set aside. Heat 2 tablespoons olive oil in a sauté pan over medium heat. Add the bread crumbs and pine nuts and cook for 1 minute. Add the shallot, garlic, and raisins and cook for 1–2 minutes or until the bread crumbs and nuts are lightly golden brown. Remove from the pan and set aside. Add the remaining 2 tablespoons olive oil and cook the cauliflower for 1–2 minutes to heat through. Add the bread crumb mixture and cook, stirring often, to coat the cauliflower. Sprinkle with lemon juice and salt and pepper to taste. Makes 4 servings.

Garlic and Scallion Smashed Potatoes

Smashed potatoes are made with waxy potatoes that hold their shape when cooked so they're ragged and chunky, not fluffy and smooth like mashed potatoes. Few recipes are easier to prepare or are more welcome than this one.

> 1½ pounds small red bliss or other waxy potatoes,
>   cut in half
> 2 tablespoons extra virgin olive oil
> 3–4 scallions, chopped
> 2 medium garlic cloves, minced
> 3 tablespoons butter or margarine
> Salt and freshly ground black pepper, to taste

Cook the potatoes in lightly salted simmering water for about 15 minutes or until fork tender. Drain the potatoes and place them in a serving bowl. Heat the olive oil in the pot used to cook the potatoes. Add the scallion and cook over low-medium heat for 2 minutes. Add the garlic and cook briefly. Add the butter and let it melt. Add the potatoes and smash them so that they are opened and crushed. Toss the ingredients to combine the potatoes with the oil-butter mixture. Season to taste with salt and pepper. Makes 4 servings.

"Smashed" means slightly crushed. **Don't mash the potatoes to smoothness. Best tools to use are a potato masher or sturdy wooden spoon.**

Green Beans with Lime Butter

Lime butter is very useful when you're making a simple dinner and need an ingredient, condiment, or other food that perks up a dish. I like it with green beans but have used it (to rave reviews) as a condiment for fish, particularly salmon, mackerel, and bluefish.

>   1 pound green beans
>   3 tablespoons butter
>   1 medium garlic clove, minced
>   1½ tablespoons lime juice
>   1 teaspoon minced fresh ginger
>   ½ teaspoon finely grated fresh lime peel
>   Salt and freshly ground black pepper, to taste

Trim the ends of the beans and rinse them. Cook the beans in lightly salted simmering water, uncovered, for 5–6 minutes or until tender. While the beans are cooking, place the butter, garlic, lime juice, ginger, lime peel, and salt and pepper to taste in a small saucepan over low-medium heat. Cook for 2–3 minutes or until the butter has melted. Drain the beans and place them in a serving dish. Add the butter sauce and toss ingredients. Makes 4 servings.

> Butter is rich and nothing tastes quite like it, but, if you want to use lime butter for a meat meal, substitute with equal amounts of pareve margarine or extra virgin olive oil.

Grilled Balsamic Vinegar–Glazed Red Onions

This recipe calls for red onions but you can also use Spanish, Bermuda, or Vidalia onions. It's a versatile dish, too: I sometimes add roasted or grilled red peppers and occasionally scatter in a few capers. For a dairy meal, blue cheese is a nice addition.

1 teaspoon fresh thyme leaves
1 teaspoon minced fresh rosemary
¼ cup balsamic vinegar
1 tablespoon extra virgin olive oil
2 large red onions, cut into ½-inch-thick slices
Salt and freshly ground black pepper, to taste

Preheat an outdoor grill or oven broiler with the rack about 6 inches from the heat source. Combine the thyme, rosemary, vinegar, and olive oil and brush the onions with some of this mixture. Sprinkle with salt and pepper. Cook the onions for 6–8 minutes per side, or until they are tender and golden brown. As the onions cook, brush them with more of the vinegar mixture, using all of the liquid. Makes 4 servings.

One of the problems with onions is that they can fall apart into rings and slip beneath the grids and into the fire of an outdoor grill. It helps if you don't peel them: the papery skins keep them together somewhat and will fall off easily once the onions are done. Use a wide, rigid spatula to turn the onions or cook them in a wire basket. Another option is to skewer the rings.

Eggplant with Yogurt and Pine Nuts

This is a deliciously comforting dish that I serve often. I like that it tastes equally fine whether it's hot, warm, or at room temperature. It's also versatile in that it is easily turned into a nondairy dish to serve with meat: eliminate the yogurt sauce and add ½ teaspoon cumin to the sautéed eggplant with the red pepper flakes.

⅓ cup pine nuts
1 cup plain yogurt
3 large garlic cloves, minced
1 teaspoon ground cumin
1 tablespoon lemon juice
½ cup extra virgin olive oil
1 medium eggplant, cut into large chunks
    (about 1½ inches)
1 medium onion, chopped
6 large plum tomatoes, cut into chunks
¼ teaspoon red pepper flakes
Salt and freshly ground black pepper, to taste

Cook the pine nuts in a dry pan over medium heat for 4–5 minutes or until lightly toasted (or heat in a toaster oven set at 350°F). Set aside. Mix the yogurt, 2 cloves minced garlic, cumin, and lemon juice in a small bowl and set aside. Heat 2 tablespoons olive oil in a sauté pan over medium heat. Add the eggplant in batches, cooking until the pieces are tender, for 6–8 minutes, adding 4 more tablespoons olive oil as needed to prevent sticking. Remove the eggplant and set aside. Add the remaining 2 tablespoons olive oil to the pan. Add the onion and cook for 2–3 minutes or until softened. Add the remaining garlic, tomatoes, red pepper flakes, eggplant, and salt and pepper to taste. Cook for about 5 minutes or until vegetables are soft. Spoon into a serving dish. Top with the pine nuts. Serve with the yogurt sauce. Serve hot, warm, or at room temperature. Makes 4 servings.

Easy Beans

When I am at a loss as to what to serve with plain grilled or roasted meat or poultry, I often fall back on this recipe. It's amazingly quick and easy to prepare and it is most forgiving: use white beans instead of black, frozen corn instead of peas, a different herb, and so on. If you like celery, you can add some (chopped) with the scallions.

¼ cup extra virgin olive oil
3–4 large scallions, coarsely chopped
1 pint small cherry tomatoes
1 cup thawed frozen peas
1 (15-ounce) can black beans, rinsed and drained
1 tablespoon minced fresh oregano (or 1 teaspoon
    dried oregano)
Salt and freshly ground black pepper, to taste

Heat the olive oil in a sauté pan over medium heat. Add the scallions and cook for about 2 minutes or until slightly softened. Add the tomatoes and peas and cook for another 2 minutes. Add the beans, oregano, and salt and pepper to taste. Cook briefly only to heat the beans through. Makes 4 servings.

Unless a recipe states otherwise, always rinse and drain canned beans.

Herb-Roasted Carrot and Parsnip "Fries"

Well, they're not french fries, of course, but they can satisfy the french fry lover in us because they have the same crispy surface feel as a potato fry. Carrots and parsnips are also sweet, so these have added—natural—sugar too. My children and grandchildren all love this dish, so I believe it is a sure way to get everyone in the family to eat vegetables.

> 1 pound carrots
> 1 pound parsnips
> 3 tablespoons extra virgin olive oil
> Salt, to taste
> 3 tablespoons minced fresh herb (or a mixture of herbs)
>> such as chives, thyme, rosemary, marjoram, parsley, oregano, and savory

Preheat the oven to 450°F. Peel the carrots and parsnips cut them into strips about 4 inches long, ½ inch wide and place in a bowl. Pour the olive oil over the vegetables and sprinkle with salt and herbs. Toss the vegetables to coat all sides and spread them onto a baking sheet. Roast for about 20 minutes, turning them once or twice, or until the vegetables are tender and lightly browned. Makes 4 servings.

Beet Greens with Red Onions and Raisins

Beets are generous vegetables. You can eat both the familiar root and the huge leaves. Some stores sell the roots and green separately; in others you can buy the entire plant. Beet roots are deliciously sweet, the greens are more nutritious. Beet greens are a particularly nice side dish with fish.

1 bunch beet greens
2 tablespoons extra virgin olive oil
¼ cup chopped red onion
2 tablespoons raisins
1 medium garlic clove, minced
½ teaspoon minced fresh ginger
1 teaspoon lemon juice
Salt, to taste

If the greens are attached to the bulbous root, cut them off (use the root for other recipes). Cut off and discard the thick stems. Wash and dry the green leaves. Heat the olive oil in a sauté pan over medium heat. Add the onion and cook for about 2 minutes. Add the raisins, garlic, and ginger and cook for a half minute. Add the beet greens and cook for about 2–3 minutes, stirring ingredients often, or until the leaves have wilted. Remove the ingredients to a serving dish and sprinkle with lemon juice and salt to taste. Makes 2–4 servings.

You can substitute spinach in this recipe. Spinach has lots of water, though, so you'll have to drain the liquid after the spinach has cooked.

Mustard-Roasted Potatoes
with Lemon-Oregano Dressing

These crispy-edged tangy morsels are a favorite in our house. They're especially good with grilled chicken or lamb. There usually aren't any leftovers unless I double the recipe, but when there are we have eaten them—rewarmed in a preheated hot oven—with eggs for breakfast.

> 2 tablespoons Dijon mustard
> 2 tablespoons extra virgin olive oil
> 1 tablespoon lemon juice
> 2 medium garlic cloves, minced
> 1 tablespoon minced fresh oregano (or 1 teaspoon
>   dried oregano)
> 1 teaspoon kosher salt, or to taste
> Freshly ground black pepper, to taste
> 1½ pounds small waxy potatoes cut into bite-size chunks

Heat the oven to 450°F. Mix the mustard with the olive oil, lemon juice, garlic, oregano, and salt and pepper to taste. Place the potatoes onto a foil-lined cookie sheet in a single layer. Pour the dressing over potatoes and toss to coat all sides completely. Roast for about 25–30 minutes, turning the potatoes occasionally, or until crispy. Makes 4–6 servings.

Waxy potatoes like red bliss, baby Yukon golds, or fingerlings have a low starch content and hold their shape well even when subjected to high heat or moisture. They are the best choices for roasting and for salad.

Roasted Asparagus with Wasabi Mayonnaise

Whether you choose fat asparagus stalks or skinny ones, roasting them is a cinch and they go with just about any meat, fish, poultry, or vegetarian entrée you can think of. You can eat roasted asparagus plain, of course, but the Wasabi Mayonnaise is a bonus. Spoon it over the stalks or use it as a dip. This recipe makes about ½ cup of the mayonnaise, which pairs well with other grilled vegetables and also grilled steak, burgers, or fish.

2 teaspoons wasabi powder
2 teaspoons water
1 pound asparagus
2 teaspoons extra virgin olive oil
Salt and freshly ground black pepper, to taste
½ cup mayonnaise
1½ teaspoons lemon juice
1 teaspoon soy sauce
¼ teaspoon sesame oil

Preheat the oven to 450°F. Mix the wasabi powder with the water to make a paste and set it aside for 5 minutes. Wash the asparagus and remove the woody bottoms. If the stalks are thick, peel the spears. Coat the asparagus with the olive oil and sprinkle with salt and pepper to taste. Lay the asparagus in a single layer on a cookie sheet. Roast for 6–12 minutes, depending on thickness, or until tender. While the asparagus is roasting, combine the mayonnaise, lemon juice, soy sauce, sesame oil, and wasabi paste and blend thoroughly. Serve the asparagus hot, warm, or cool with the wasabi mayonnaise. Makes 4 servings.

If you have Gold's Wasabi Sauce on hand, you can use it (one tablespoon) instead of the wasabi paste.

Wasabi is the greenish condiment served with sushi. It comes from the root of an Asian plant and is often called Japanese horseradish, although it is a member of the cabbage family and its pungency is reminiscent of hot mustard. Wasabi's robust flavor makes it a tasty partner for many foods other than sushi. To make the dried powdered form into a paste, mix it with water. Wasabi powders are sometimes not 100 percent wasabi; they may also include regular horseradish and mustard.

Roasted Plum Tomatoes

This dish is delightfully versatile and one I make often because it goes with a wide variety of foods from grilled, roasted, or baked fish, chicken, beef, or lamb to meatless dishes such as Bulgur Wheat with Lentils, Caramelized Onions, and Mushrooms (page 67), salads such as Potato-Corn Salad with Basil Vinaigrette (page 62) or other vegetable dishes such as Garlic and Onion Smashed Potatoes (page 182) or Herb-Roasted Carrot and Parsnip "Fries" (page 187). It will also add bright color to a dinner plate. All that plus it tastes wonderful whether you serve it hot, warm, or at room temperature.

> 10 large plum tomatoes
> 4 large garlic cloves, minced
> 3 tablespoons fresh or dried bread crumbs
> 2 tablespoons minced fresh basil
> 2 tablespoons minced fresh parsley
> 3 tablespoons extra virgin olive oil
> Salt and freshly ground black pepper, to taste

Preheat the oven to 425°F. Cut the tomatoes in half lengthwise and place them cut side up in a baking dish large enough to hold them in a single layer. Scatter the garlic on top. Sprinkle with the bread crumbs, basil, and parsley. Drizzle the olive oil on top and season to taste with salt and pepper. Roast for 25–30 minutes or until the tomatoes are soft and the bread crumbs are crispy. Makes 4–6 servings.

Pan-Fried Paprika Potatoes

Paprika is a powder made by grinding dried peppers (including red bell and chile peppers). There are hot and sweet varieties and a Spanish-style smoky-flavored paprika. All give a rich russet color to food, which is why paprika has been used so often as a garnish. But it's a robust spice that packs lots of flavor too.

> 2–2½ pounds Yukon gold potatoes, cut into medium
>   chunks
> 3 tablespoons extra virgin olive oil
> 3 tablespoons butter or margarine
> 1 medium onion, chopped
> 1 teaspoon sweet paprika
> Salt, to taste

Place the potatoes in a saucepan, cover with lightly salted water, and bring to a boil over high heat. Lower the heat and cook for about 10 minutes or until they are barely tender. Drain the potatoes and peel them, if desired, when cool enough to handle. Heat the olive oil and butter in sauté pan over medium-high heat. When the butter has melted and looks foamy, add the potatoes and cook for about 8 minutes, stirring occasionally or until they are beginning to brown. Reduce the heat to medium. Add the onion and toss the ingredients gently to distribute them evenly. Sprinkle with paprika and salt to taste. Continue to cook, stirring occasionally, for 8–10 minutes or until potatoes are browned and crusty. Makes 4–6 servings.

Paprika contains a good amount of vitamin C. Its relatively high natural sugar content means it may burn easily when cooked. When preparing foods with paprika, don't use high heat for too long and be sure the contents of the pan are moist. As with all spices, be sure to keep paprika in a tightly covered container in a dark place away from the heat. Flavor and color deteriorate after 6–8 months, although you can still use the spice for a few more months.

Sautéed Brussels Sprouts with Onions

When I was first married my husband, Ed told me that there were two things he would never eat. One of them was Brussels sprouts. But I made this recipe once and he loved it. Now, even he has become a fan of this much-maligned vegetable. During the autumn and winter when Brussels sprouts are at their peak, we probably eat this dish once a week at our house.

> 18–24 fresh Brussels sprouts
> 3 tablespoons extra virgin olive oil
> 1 Vidalia or large yellow onion, chopped
> Salt and freshly ground black pepper, to taste

Rinse the Brussels sprouts and trim the bottoms. Cut the sprouts in half or, if they are very large, into quarters. Heat the olive oil in a sauté pan over medium heat, add the sprouts, onion, and salt and pepper to taste. Cook, covered, for 3 minutes, stirring the vegetables once or twice during that time. Remove the cover and cook for 4–5 minutes or until the vegetables are tender. Makes 4 servings.

It's easy to vary this dish so that you can serve it often:

- Use red onion.
- Add some fresh thyme leaves.
- Add mustard seeds or poppy seeds.
- Scatter in some freshly grated lemon peel and a few drops of lemon juice.

Sautéed Carrots with Mint and Shallots

Shallots and garlic make everyday carrots more interesting and mint adds a light, refreshing quality. This recipe is perfect with Boneless Lamb with Cumin and Ginger (page 104), Grilled Turkish-Style Cornish Hens (page 145), Boneless Broiled Turkey London Broil with Chipotle Pesto (page 137), and plain grilled meats or poultry.

> 8 medium carrots
> 2 tablespoons extra virgin olive oil
> 2 large shallots, about ¼ cup chopped
> 2 medium garlic cloves, minced
> 2 tablespoons minced fresh mint
> Salt and freshly ground black pepper, to taste

Wash the carrots and cut them into ½-inch-thick slices. Cook, covered, in lightly salted simmering water for about 5 minutes or until the carrots are tender but firm. Drain under cold water and set aside. Heat the olive oil in a sauté pan over medium heat. Add the shallots and cook for 1–2 minutes to soften them slightly. Add the garlic and cook briefly. Add the carrots, mint, and salt and pepper to taste. Cook for about 2 minutes or until the carrots are hot and slightly crispy on the surface. Makes 4 servings.

If you buy carrots with the leaves intact, cut the leaves off and discard them. The leaves leech the moisture out of the orange root.

Parsnip and Potato Puree

This is a thick, creamy, fluffy dish that tastes like a sweeter version of mashed potatoes. Make it with butter and milk and serve it with fish; switch to margarine and soy milk and use it as a bed for grilled steak. I like this with Pepper-Crusted Bluefish with Horseradish Yogurt Sauce (page 94), because the mellow flavor is a good balance for the robust sauce that accompanies the fish, but also like it with Chicken in the Pot with Pears, Dried Figs, and Cider (page 125), because sugary qualities in both work harmoniously together.

> 1 pound parsnips, sliced ½ inch thick
> 1 pound Yukon gold or all-purpose potatoes, peeled and
>   cut into 1-inch chunks
> 2 McIntosh or other crisp, tart apples, peeled, cored, and
>   cut into chunks
> ¼ cup butter or margarine
> ½ cup milk or unflavored soy milk
> Salt and freshly ground black pepper, to taste

Cook the parsnips and potatoes in lightly salted boiling water for 10 minutes. Add the apples, lower the heat, and cook for another 5 minutes or until the parsnips and potatoes are tender. Drain the ingredients and return them to the pan. Add the butter and mash it into the other ingredients. Continue to mash, adding the milk gradually, until the ingredients form a smooth puree. Taste for seasoning and add salt and pepper to taste. Makes 4–6 servings.

Spinach with Garlic, Chile Pepper, and Lemon

This is another dish we eat often at our house because it goes with almost everything. I don't always include the chile pepper.

> 2 bunches fresh spinach
> 2 tablespoons extra virgin olive oil
> 2 garlic cloves, minced
> ⅛ teaspoon red pepper flakes (or a small dry
>   red chile pepper)
> Salt, to taste
> Few drops of lemon juice

Wash and dry the spinach. Heat the olive oil in a sauté pan over medium heat. Add the garlic and cook briefly. Add the spinach and cook, turning with tongs to move the raw leaves to the bottom, for 2–3 minutes or until wilted. Add the red pepper flakes and salt to taste. Stir, then sprinkle with a few drops of lemon juice. Makes 4 servings.

A garlic press can be a home cook's good friend. You can use it whenever you need minced garlic. Be sure to press the garlic cloves over a small bowl or other receptacle so you don't lose any of the precious juices that squirt out.

Stir-Fried Broccoli
with Orange Peel and Red Chile Peppers

Broccoli never tasted so good! It's a sturdy, robust vegetable with a distinctive taste but the orange peel and chile peppers stand up to it as equals, bringing several tastes to your mouth all at once. This dish is works well as an accompaniment for plain grilled, broiled, or roasted meats, poultry, or fish.

> 1 bunch broccoli
> 2½ tablespoons vegetable oil
> ½ teaspoon salt
> ¼ cup orange juice
> 1 large garlic clove, minced
> 2 scallions, chopped
> 2 teaspoons minced fresh ginger
> 2 dried red chile peppers
> 2 teaspoons finely grated fresh orange peel
> 1 teaspoon sesame oil

Clean and cut the broccoli stems and florets. Heat 2 tablespoons oil in a wok, stir-fry pan, or sauté pan over medium heat. Add the broccoli and stir-fry for 2 minutes. Add the salt and orange juice. Cover the pan and cook for 2 minutes. Dish out the broccoli and set aside. Drain the liquid but reserve it. Return the pan to the heat. Add the remaining ½ tablespoon oil. Add the garlic, scallions, ginger, chile peppers, and grated orange peel and stir-fry for 2 minutes. Return the reserved liquid to the pan and cook to evaporate most of it. Return the broccoli to the pan and stir-fry until the broccoli is tender and heated through. Add sesame oil, stir-fry to blend it in and serve. Makes 4 servings.

Stir-Fried Fennel

Fennel is more versatile than you might think. It tastes wonderful when it's still slightly crispy and resilient, but I like to keep cooking this dish until the vegetable is soft and brown. It all depends on how much time I have. The final flourish of lemon juice is also up to you. Cut off a piece of lemon and squirt as much juice as you like over the finished vegetable.

> 2 bulbs fennel
> 2 tablespoons extra virgin olive oil
> Salt and freshly ground black pepper, to taste
> 1 teaspoon fresh thyme leaves, optional
> Few drops of lemon juice

Remove the stalks and frilly fronds from the fennel. Cut the bulbs into quarters and cut the quarters into ¼-inch-thick slices. Heat the olive oil in a wok, stir-fry pan, or sauté pan over medium heat. Add the fennel and stir-fry for 3–4 minutes. Sprinkle with salt, pepper, and thyme, if using. Pour in 2 tablespoons water, cover the pan, and cook for 2–3 minutes. Remove the cover and continue to cook for another 3–4 minutes or until the fennel is lightly brown, longer if you like it soft and golden brown. Sprinkle some lemon juice on top. Makes 4 servings.

> Fennel's feathery fronds are beautiful as a garnish for other foods.

Sweet Potato Pancakes

There's always been some confusion about yams and sweet potatoes in this country. What we eat are sweet potatoes, native to the American tropics (even though they may be called yams in the store). The vegetable resembles the African *nyami*, which is a completely different species and not produced commercially here. There are several varieties of sweet potatoes available. Some are dark, some pale fleshed. Try them all to see which you prefer.

> 2 medium sweet potatoes, about 1½ pounds, peeled
> ½ cup raisins
> 2 tablespoons all-purpose flour
> 2 large eggs
> ½ teaspoon salt
> ¼ teaspoon ground cinnamon
> ¼ teaspoon freshly grated nutmeg
> ¼ teaspoon baking powder
> Vegetable oil for frying

Shred the potatoes in a food processor. Place the potatoes in a rigid strainer set over a bowl and press to squeeze out as much liquid as possible (or squeeze in a towel). Put the potatoes in a large bowl. Stir in the raisins, flour, eggs, salt, cinnamon, nutmeg, and baking powder. Heat about ⅛ inch vegetable oil in a cast-iron or other heavy heat-retaining pan. Scoop enough of the pancake mixture to form pancakes about 3 inches in diameter and ¼ inch thick. Before shaping, squeeze the mixture to extract as much liquid as possible. Fry the pancakes in batches over moderately high heat for 2–3 minutes per side or until the pancakes are golden brown and crispy. Drain on paper towels. Makes 4 servings.

The raisins can fall out of the pancakes because the mixture is not a typical batter. When you place the pancakes in the pan, press the raisins down into the sweet potato shreds. If you don't like raisins you can substitute dried cranberries, which will give the pancakes more of a tart taste. Or simply leave the raisins out! The pancakes will still be sweet, crispy, and delicious.

Zucchini Fritters

Fritters are crispy foods that have welcoming qualities. These are light, even though they're fried and you can eat them hot, warm or cool. Serve the fritters as a part of a dairy meal or as hors d'oeuvres. They also go well with dishes such as Baked Grouper with Tomatoes and Herbs (page 87), Broiled Branzini with Tomato-Olive Relish (page 85), or Pan-Seared Tilapia with Lemon, Shallots, and Browned Butter (page 95).

> 2 medium zucchini, about 12–16 ounces
> Salt, about ½ teaspoon
> 2 scallions, minced
> 1 small onion, chopped
> ¼ cup minced fresh dill
> ½ cup crumbled feta cheese
> 2 large eggs, beaten
> Freshly ground black pepper, to taste
> ⅔ cup all-purpose flour
> Vegetable oil for frying
> Plain yogurt or dairy sour cream, if desired

Shred the zucchini in a food processor. Transfer the shreds to a colander, sprinkle with salt and let rest for 10 minutes. Press the shreds to squeeze out as much liquid as possible. Place the shreds in a bowl and add the scallions, onion, dill, cheese, eggs, and pepper to taste. Mix the ingredients thoroughly. Add the flour and blend it in. Pour about ¼ inch of vegetable oil into a large sauté pan over medium-high heat. For each fritter, drop about ⅛ cup of the zucchini batter into the pan and flatten it slightly. Leave plenty of room between fritters. Fry for about 2 minutes per side or until golden brown and crispy. Drain on paper towels. Repeat with the remaining batter. Serve plain or with plain yogurt or dairy sour cream. Makes 4–6 servings.

> Foods fried too close together will steam as they fry and become soggy. It's important to leave plenty of space between the pieces.

DESSERTS

Desserts are not an everyday item at our house. Like almost everyone else we know, we are always trying to limit calories, forego sweets, and avoid too much fat. Unfortunately, many of our favorite goodies are loaded with all of those, so foods such as ice cream, cake, and fudge sauce are treated as . . . treats. We eat them occasionally, so that desserts have become even more special.

The kosher cook faces an additional consideration. Choosing the appropriate dessert is not just about diet and health, but also whether the recipe is dairy or pareve. After eating meat or poultry, it is usually necessary to wait six hours before eating dairy.

The dessert recipes here include some dairy, some pareve. Banana and Honeyed-Fudge Sauce Sundaes (page 203) and Pomegranate Ice Cream Alaskas (page 212) are meant to follow a dairy meal; desserts like Tropical Ambrosia with Chile-Lime Syrup (page 217), Clove and Lemongrass–Poached Plums (page 221), and Spiced Oranges (page 220) are perfect after meat or poultry.

Some of the dairy-based dessert recipes can be converted to pareve. Mexican Hot Chocolate Brownies (page 210), Blueberry Crisp with Cereal Crust (page 205), or The Grand Finale (page 222)—the cookie with everything—call for butter but you can switch to pareve margarine. Of course, substituting goes only so far! Obviously, desserts like Berry-Cheese Tart (page 204), which includes butter, mascarpone cheese, cream cheese, and dairy sour cream, would take some doing and wouldn't taste anything like the real thing if nondairy substitutes were used.

I've specified using unsalted butter in the recipes here that call for butter. While I think unsalted butter is always preferable because it tastes fresher and lets you decide how much salt you want to add to a dish, it is particularly important for dessert recipes to maintain a good balance of sweet and salty.

Many of the dessert recipes are attractive and festive enough for company dinners. But they are all fairly quick and easy to prepare, so you can make them for family when it's time for a special treat during the busy week.

Banana and Honeyed-Fudge Sauce Sundaes

When was the last time you had an old-fashioned hot fudge sundae? The sauce on this one is smooth and not cloyingly sweet—you can use it for all sorts of desserts.

1 tablespoon unsalted butter
1 tablespoon honey
½ cup whipping cream
4 ounces bittersweet chocolate, coarsely chopped
4 small or 2 large bananas
4 scoops vanilla ice cream
1½ cups crumbled cinnamon graham crackers, macaroons, or biscotti

Place the butter, honey, and cream in a small saucepan over medium heat until the butter has melted and bubbles form around the edges of the pan. Stir in the chocolate and remove the pan from the heat. Whisk the ingredients until the chocolate has melted and the sauce is smooth. Let cool. Slice the bananas in half lengthwise and place in each of four dessert plates (if using large bananas cut each in half crosswise first and then proceed). Top with the ice cream. Pour the fudge sauce on top. Scatter with the cookie crumbs. Makes 4 servings.

Berry-Cheese Tart

So easy! You don't even have to cook this dish, yet it is elegant and delicious and looks as if you've fussed. The oatmeal cookie crust is rich and mellow tasting but you can substitute a graham cracker or chocolate crumb crust if you prefer. When you shop for the berries, use whichever look freshest: raspberries, strawberries, blackberries, blueberries—they are all fine (and you can use apricot jam instead of raspberry if you wish).

1⅓ cups oatmeal cookie crumbs
4 tablespoons melted unsalted butter
8 ounces mascarpone cheese
4 ounces cream cheese
⅓ cup dairy sour cream
6 tablespoons sugar
1 tablespoon lemon juice
¾ teaspoon vanilla extract
2 half-pints raspberries
2 tablespoons seedless raspberry jam

Mix the cookie crumbs and melted butter thoroughly. Press evenly onto the bottom and sides of a 9-inch tart pan. Chill for at least 1 hour. Mix the mascarpone cheese, cream cheese, dairy sour cream, sugar, lemon juice, and vanilla extract until smooth and uniform. Spoon the filling into the oatmeal crust and spread it evenly. Chill for at least 1 hour. Before serving, arrange the berries on top of the tart. Melt the jam and brush lightly on top of the berries. Makes 8 servings.

You won't be able to buy packaged **oatmeal cookie crumbs; you'll have to make your own in a food processor or blender. There are several kosher brands of raisin-free oatmeal cookies available.**

Among the must-have tools in your kitchen **are pastry brushes. You'll need three or four of them for brushing jam onto berries, barbecue sauce onto meat, olive oil onto baking sheets, and so many countless other tasks that you'll wonder how you ever did without them. My preference is to use nylon brushes, because they are soft, for ingredients like jam, to be brushed onto delicate items such as berries in this recipe. I like the firmer silicone brushes for heavier uses such as brushing vegetable oil onto cookie sheets or barbecue sauce onto meat or poultry.**

Blueberry Crisp with Cereal Crust

This is a favorite in the spring and summer when fresh blueberries are available. But I use the crunchy crust as a top for all sorts of fruit cobblers throughout the year. You can embellish this dessert by adding a cut-up peach or nectarine.

Filling

2 pints fresh blueberries

⅓ cup sugar

5 tablespoons all-purpose flour

¼ teaspoon ground cinnamon

2 tablespoons lemon juice

Crust

1 cup bran flakes or raisin bran flakes

½ cup quick-cooking or rolled oats

½ cup chopped nuts such as almonds, cashews, or pecans

¼ cup brown sugar

½ teaspoon ground cinnamon

6 tablespoons melted unsalted butter or margarine

Preheat the oven to 350°F. Combine the blueberries, sugar, flour, ¼ teaspoon cinnamon, and lemon juice in a 6-quart baking dish. Set aside. Crush the bran flakes slightly and put them in a bowl. Add the oats, nuts, brown sugar, and ½ teaspoon cinnamon and toss ingredients to distribute them evenly. Pour in the melted butter. Mix until the dry the ingredients are coated with the melted butter. Spread the cereal mixture over the fruit. Bake for 30 minutes or until the crust is crispy and brown. Let cool slightly but serve warm (may be rewarmed). Serve plain or with ice cream, whipped cream, or sorbet. Makes 6–8 servings.

Both quick-cooking or rolled oats are fine for crisp and cobbler crusts. If you use quick oats, the crust will be softer; rolled oats will yield a firmer texture.

Double-Chocolate Pudding and Granola Parfait

Here's an old-fashioned dessert that takes about as much time as the boxed kind, but has all natural ingredients and no preservatives. Unlike boxed pudding, this is also enriched with extra chocolate. You can serve the pudding plain or with some whipped cream, but if you have more time, it can become a more elaborate parfait with a simple "granola" topping and some whipped cream. In that case, make the granola first so you can layer the ingredients properly.

Double-Chocolate Pudding

3 cups milk
⅔ cup sugar
⅓ cup cocoa powder
⅓ cup cornstarch
¼ teaspoon salt
3 ounces semisweet chocolate
1½ teaspoons vanilla extract

Bring 2½ cups milk to a simmer in a saucepan over medium heat (bubbles should form around the edges). While the milk is heating, sift the sugar, cocoa powder, cornstarch, and salt into a bowl. Pour in the remaining ½ cup of milk and whisk ingredients until they are well blended. Whisk the hot milk in gradually. Return the ingredients to the pan. Add the semisweet chocolate and cook over medium heat for 2–3 minutes, stirring constantly, or until the mixture begins to bubble and is thick and smooth. Remove from the heat and stir in the vanilla extract. Pour into individual dessert dishes. Makes 6 servings.

Granola Parfait

¼ cup all-purpose flour

¼ cup quick-cooking oats

⅓ finely chopped toasted almonds

¼ cup dried flaked coconut

2 tablespoons brown sugar

4 tablespoons unsalted butter

½ cup whipping cream

1 teaspoon sugar

Shaved semisweet chocolate

Preheat the oven to 350°F. Mix the flour, oats, almonds, coconut and brown sugar. Work in the butter until the mixture is well combined and crumbly. Place on a cookie sheet and bake for 12–15 minutes. Let cool. Whip the cream with the sugar until thick. Place some granola in each of 6–8 parfait or dessert dishes, top with some Double Chocolate Pudding. Repeat the layers. Add the whipped cream as the top layer. Garnish with chocolate shavings. Makes 6–8 servings.

To make whipped cream, pour the cream into a large metal bowl (or the bowl of a standing mixer) and add the sugar. Whip with a hand beater (or the whisk attachment of a standing mixer), starting at slow speed and gradually increasing to high speed. Whip until the cream stands in soft but definite peaks. For best results, place the bowl in the refrigerator for 10–15 minutes before proceeding with the recipe.

The granola is a sweet, crunchy topping you can also use on top of yogurt or ice cream.

Lemon-Ginger Shortcakes with Berries

The word *short* (in shortcake and shortbread) is an old English cooking term that means "crisp," but shortcakes are a quintessentially American dessert. The combination of cool tender fruit, soft, sweet whipped cream, and crispy biscuits is irresistible. The biscuits in this recipe are incredibly easy to make—they're drop biscuits, so you don't have to roll the dough. You simply drop blobs of dough onto cookie sheets to bake. When I want to serve plain breakfast biscuits, I use this recipe but leave out the ginger. Biscuits are always best when freshly made but you can bake them ahead and store them in the freezer in a plastic bag.

> 1 quart fresh strawberries or mixed berries
> 3 tablespoons plus 1 teaspoon sugar
> 2 cups all-purpose flour
> ¾ teaspoon salt
> 2½ teaspoons baking powder
> 1 tablespoon finely grated fresh lemon peel
> 2 tablespoons chopped crystallized ginger
> 6 tablespoons unsalted butter, cut into small pieces
> 1 large egg
> ¾ cup milk
> 1 cup whipping cream

Preheat the oven to 450°F. Slice the berries, sprinkle them with 2 tablespoons sugar, and set aside in a bowl. In another bowl, mix the flour, 1 tablespoon sugar, salt, and baking powder. Add the lemon peel, crystallized ginger, and butter and work into the dry ingredients until the mixture resembles coarse meal. In a small bowl, beat the egg and milk together with a fork until well combined. Add to the flour mixture and mix until a soft, sticky dough forms. Drop 6–8 equal mounds of the dough onto an ungreased cookie sheet. Bake for about 12–15 minutes or until puffed and lightly brown. Let cool. Whip the cream with the remaining 1 teaspoon sugar until the mixture stands in soft peaks but is still slightly pourable. To assemble the dessert, cut the biscuits in half and place each bottom half on a serving dish. Place the berries on top. Pour some of the cream on top. Top with the remaining biscuit halves. Makes 6–8 servings.

Prepare the berries first so they can moisten and soften as they absorb the sugar.

If you use blackberries, cut them in half; leave raspberries whole. You can crush some of the berries to let their natural juices seep into the biscuit.

Mango Fool

This is a particularly refreshing dessert on a hot day or after a spicy meal. It's really easy to make and you can transform it into a glamorous dessert for company by spooning portions of the fool into meringue or cake shells, baked mini-pie crusts, or cookie crusts (top the fool with toasted coconut).

        2 large ripe mangoes
        2 teaspoons minced fresh ginger
        3 tablespoons honey
        ½ cup plain yogurt
        1 cup whipping cream
        Fresh mint sprigs

Peel and pit the mangoes and cut the flesh into chunks. Puree the chunks with the ginger in a food processor. Stir in the honey and yogurt. Pour the cream into a large metal bowl (or the bowl of a standing mixer). Whip with a hand beater (or the whisk attachment of a standing mixer), starting at slow speed and gradually increasing to high speed. Whip until thick. Fold into the mango mixture. Refrigerate until chilled. Garnish with mint sprigs. Makes 4–6 servings.

Mexican Hot Chocolate Brownies

The culinary pairing of chile peppers and chocolate comes from ancient civilizations in South America, Mexico, and what is now the American southwest. It has endured for centuries so it's obviously a winning combination! These brownies will keep everyone guessing as to what that extra flavor could be.

4 ounces unsweetened chocolate
6 tablespoons unsalted butter or margarine
2 large eggs
1 cup sugar
⅔ cup all-purpose flour
½ teaspoon ground cinnamon
¼ teaspoon pure ancho chile powder
¼ teaspoon salt
1 teaspoon vanilla extract
½ cup chocolate chips

Preheat the oven to 350°F. Lightly grease an 8-inch square baking pan. Put the chocolate and butter in the top part of a double boiler set over barely simmering water. Cook for 3–4 minutes or until the ingredients have melted. Stir the ingredients together. Remove the top part of the double boiler from the heat. Combine the eggs and sugar in a large bowl and beat them with an electric mixer set at medium speed for 2–3 minutes or until the mixture has thickened. Add the flour, cinnamon, chile powder, salt, vanilla extract, and chocolate chips and stir them in. Add the chocolate and butter mixture and stir to blend all the ingredients thoroughly. Pour the batter into the prepared pan. Bake for 28–30 minutes or until a cake tester inserted into the center comes out with a few crumbs clinging. Cool the brownies in the pan. Cut into 16 pieces. Makes 16 pieces.

Look carefully at the label on the jar of chile powder to be sure you are using pure chile powder. Most generic chile powders are blends of ground dried chiles plus cumin, oregano, salt, and other ingredients. Pure chile powder (usually ancho chile) contains no other flavorings.

Crunchy Almond-Apple Cake

This cake has a tender bottom, crunchy crust, and a layer of soft fruit in between. The textures are so intriguing that you'll nibble at this cake every time you pass it by. Until it's gone.

2 Granny Smith or other tart apples
¾ cup unsalted butter
1 cup sugar
2 large eggs
2 cups all-purpose flour
2 teaspoons baking powder
¾ teaspoon salt
½ teaspoon almond extract

Topping

6 tablespoons unsalted butter or margarine
½ cup sugar
1 tablespoon all-purpose flour
1 cup chopped almonds

Preheat the oven to 350°F. Lightly grease a 9-inch springform pan. Peel, core, and chop the apples into ½-inch chunks and set aside. Place the ¾ cup butter and 1 cup sugar together in a large bowl and cream them with an electric mixer set at medium speed for 3 minutes or until they are fluffy and smooth. Add the eggs and beat them in thoroughly. Add the 2 cups flour, baking powder, salt, and almond extract and blend them in. Spoon the batter into the prepared pan. Arrange the apples over the batter. Bake for 40 minutes. While the cake is baking, heat the 6 tablespoons butter and ½ cup sugar together in a small saucepan over medium heat. When the butter has melted, stir in the 1 tablespoon flour and almonds. Set aside. After the cake has baked 40 minutes, spoon the topping over the partially baked cake. Return the cake to the oven and bake for 20 minutes longer, or until top is golden brown. Let the cake cool in the pan for about 15 minutes. Remove the sides of the pan and let the cake cool or serve it slightly warm. Makes 6–8 servings.

Pomegranate Ice Cream Alaskas

You've got to think ahead if you want to make these! Even though this dessert is easy to make and takes almost no time to put together, there's some freezing time to consider. Baked Alaska is a time-honored dessert, the stuff of old-fashioned cruise-ship galas. But after all, it's just ice cream, cake, and meringue, so it's also perfectly suitable for a special family dinner or for company. The ice cream flavor is a bit different than usual, and will keep everyone guessing. Of course you can skip the cake and meringue part and just have the ice cream!

> 2 cups vanilla ice cream
> ¼ cup pomegranate paste
> 4 store-bought chocolate or graham cracker crust
>   tart shells
> 2 large egg whites
> ¼ cup sugar

Remove the ice cream from the freezer to let soften (about 15 minutes). Mix the ice cream and pomegranate paste until well blended and uniform in color. Return the ice cream to the freezer and let harden. Preheat the oven to 450°F. Scoop equal amounts of the ice cream into each of the tart shells. Return the filled shells to the freezer until the ice cream is firm. When the ice cream is firm, beat the egg whites in a large bowl using an electric mixer set on medium. Gradually increase to high speed and beat until the egg whites stand in soft peaks. Continue to beat, gradually adding the sugar, until the whites stand in stiff peaks. Spread the meringue over each tart, piling it high and sealing the edges where the tart crumbs and ice cream meet. Place the tarts on a cookie sheet and bake for 2–3 minutes or until the meringue is lightly brown. Makes 4 servings.

It's simple to make all sorts of interesting flavors out of plain vanilla ice cream. If you don't want pomegranate, try spice ice cream: for each 2 cups of vanilla ice cream, stir in 1 teaspoon freshly grated nutmeg and ½ teaspoon ground coriander.

Egg whites whip best when they are at room temperature.

Roasted Peaches with Fresh Herbs

Sweet, juicy, ripe summer peaches are good enough for dessert without doing anything. But sometimes just a touch of this or that can make plain fruit into a stunning dessert that becomes a wonderful surprise after dinner. These roasted peaches, lightly sugared, rich with butter, and with just a hint of herbs dazzle in their simplicity and flavor. Making them is effortless, too.

> 4 ripe freestone peaches
> 2 tablespoons melted unsalted butter
> 4 teaspoons brown sugar
> 1½ teaspoons minced fresh mint
> 1 teaspoon minced fresh lemon verbena or rosemary

Preheat the oven to 450°F. Cut the peaches in half and remove and discard the pits. Brush the peaches with the melted butter. Place the peaches cut side up in a baking pan. Sprinkle with the sugar. Sprinkle on the herbs. Roast for 5 minutes. Turn the peaches over. Roast for another 3–7 minutes, or until tender when pierced with the tip of a sharp knife. Let cool to warm or room temperature. Serve plain or with vanilla ice cream or lemon sorbet. Makes 4 servings.

Flourless Chocolate Cake

There are so many recipes for flourless chocolate cakes but this one has a double-chocolatey goodness, combining semisweet chocolate and cocoa, plus a double dose of coffee for an intense, rich taste. The cake looks plain, but wait until you bite into it! It's dense, moist, and lavish.

8 ounces semisweet chocolate
1 tablespoon instant coffee powder
1 cup unsalted butter or margarine
5 large eggs
1 cup sugar
¾ cup unsweetened cocoa powder
2 tablespoons cold coffee
Confectioners' sugar, whipped cream, or ice cream, optional

Preheat the oven to 350°F. Lightly grease a 9- or 10-inch springform pan. Place a parchment paper circle on the bottom of the pan and grease the paper. Put the chocolate, instant coffee powder, and butter in the top of a double boiler set over barely simmering water and cook until the chocolate has melted, stirring occasionally to blend ingredients completely. Remove the top of the double boiler from the heat. Let cool slightly. Combine the eggs, sugar, and cocoa powder in a large bowl and beat with an electric mixer set at medium speed for 2–3 minutes or until well blended, scraping down the sides of the bowl once or twice. Add the chocolate mixture and cold coffee and blend them in thoroughly. Pour the batter into the prepared pan. Bake for 35–40 minutes or until a cake tester inserted into the center comes out with a few chocolate crumbs clinging to the sides. Transfer to a cake rack to cool. Cut around the edges of the cake with the tip of a knife. Release the sides of the springform pan. Invert onto a cake plate. Remove the parchment paper. Serve plain or dusted with confectioners' sugar or accompanied by whipped cream or ice cream. Makes 10–12 servings.

If you bake regularly and have room in your kitchen, you might want to invest in a good standing mixer. If that's out of the question, buy a good hand mixer with lots of power and sturdy, wiry beaters that don't have a center post.

You can buy parchment paper circles in cookware stores.

Sautéed Balsamic-Glazed Pears
with Gorgonzola Cheese and Walnuts

Of all the well-known, well-loved culinary duos, pears and blue-veined cheeses are right at the top. This recipe is a bit glamorous, so you can save it for company, but it's easy enough to make, so why not treat the family? You can cook the pears and the sauce the day before—bring the fruit to room temperature and reheat the glaze gently over low heat.

½ cup orange juice
⅓ cup balsamic vinegar
2 tablespoons honey
2 large firm pears
Half of a lemon
2 tablespoons unsalted butter
8 whole meal crackers (or use 4 oatmeal cookies)
2 ounces Gorgonzola cheese
3 tablespoons chopped walnuts

Heat the orange juice, vinegar, and honey in a small saucepan over high heat. Bring to a boil and simmer for 8–10 minutes or until it has reduced to a thin syrupy consistency (it will thicken more as it cools). Set aside to cool. Peel, halve, and core the pears and rub them with the cut side of the lemon. Cut the halves to make quarters. Heat the butter in a sauté pan over medium heat. When the butter has melted and looks foamy, add the pears and cook for about 2–3 minutes or until they are glazed and lightly browned and have softened slightly. Remove from the heat. Place the crackers on each of four dessert plates. Place two pear quarters on each of the plates. Add a chunk of Gorgonzola cheese to each plate. Pour the glaze over the pears. Sprinkle the nuts on top. This may be served warm or at room temperature. Makes 4 servings.

The best pears for sautéing include the sweet and juicy Comice, Bartlett, and Anjou. Pears are almost always rock hard when you buy them. Let them ripen and soften for a day or so at room temperature. They should be tender but not too soft or they'll fall apart when you cook them.

Cinnamon Fudgies

These little bites of fudge cookies with just a hint of cinnamon have an elegant look, but they're good for dunking, too. You can freeze them for a month or two in a plastic bag.

> 8 ounces semisweet chocolate
> 1 tablespoon unsalted butter or margarine
> 2 large eggs
> ¾ cup sugar
> ¼ cup all-purpose flour
> ¼ teaspoon baking powder
> ¼ teaspoon ground cinnamon
> Pinch or two of salt
> ¾ teaspoon vanilla extract
> ⅔ cup finely chopped nuts such as walnuts, pecans,
>   almonds, or cashews

Preheat the oven to 350°F. Put the chocolate and butter together in the top of a double boiler set over barely simmering water and cook, stirring occasionally, until the chocolate has melted. Remove the top of the double boiler from the heat. Let cool slightly. Place the eggs in a mixing bowl and beat them with an electric mixer set at medium speed, gradually adding the sugar, until the mixture is thick and light yellow, about 4 minutes. Stir in the chocolate mixture. Add flour, baking powder, cinnamon, and salt and blend in thoroughly. Stir in the vanilla extract and the nuts. Drop the batter by the teaspoonful onto a lightly greased cookie sheet. Bake for about 10 minutes or until top is glossy and cookies are set. Makes about 3 dozen.

If you bake cookies with any regularity, consider buying silicone baking sheets or parchment paper, which are naturally "nonstick" and obviate the need for greasing cookie sheets. Parchment paper can be used for every type of cookie. Silicone sheets are thick and may prevent proper browning of crispy cookies, but are perfect for delicate cookies and those that don't require deep browning. Silicone's big advantage is that it wipes clean with a damp sponge and can be used thousands of times.

Tropical Ambrosia
with Chile-Lime Syrup

Ambrosia is an old-fashioned Southern fruit dessert that made its first appearance in American cookbooks in the last part of the nineteenth century. There were variations on the recipe but all included orange sections and grated coconut. This contemporary version also has mango and pineapple for the spicy, acidic flavors they offer, grapes for added color, and a faintly spicy-hot honey-lime dressing.

1 mango
2 navel oranges
½ pineapple
1 cup red seedless grapes, cut in half
1 cup shredded coconut
¼ cup honey
3 tablespoons lime juice
⅛ teaspoon cayenne pepper

Peel the mango and cut the flesh into chunks. Place the chunks in a bowl. Peel the orange and cut it into thick slices across the sections. Remove the white pith from the outer edge and cut the oranges into chunks. Add to the bowl. Remove the shell, cut the pineapple into chunks, and add the pieces and the grapes and coconut to the bowl. Toss the fruit. In a small bowl blend the honey and lime juice and pour over the fruit. Sprinkle with the cayenne pepper. Toss ingredients. Spoon into serving bowls. Let rest for about 10 minutes before serving. Makes 4 servings.

Yogurt Spice Cake

This is an all-purpose coffee cake that's just right for those times when you want something plain for dessert or as a snack during the day. The Yogurt Sauce dresses it up a bit but the cake is fine just plain. I also make the Yogurt Sauce to use with fresh fruit when I want something extra, but simple and easy to make.

1 ¾ cups all-purpose flour

1 teaspoon ground cinnamon

1 teaspoon freshly grated nutmeg

½ teaspoon ground allspice

½ teaspoon ground ginger

½ teaspoon salt

1 teaspoon baking powder

1 teaspoon baking soda

1 cup sugar

½ cup unsalted butter

2 large eggs

1 cup plain yogurt

Preheat the oven to 350°F. Butter and flour an 8-inch square cake pan. Whisk the flour, cinnamon, nutmeg, allspice, ginger, salt, baking powder, and baking soda in a bowl. Set aside. Place the sugar and butter in a large bowl and cream them with an electric mixer set at medium speed for 3 minutes or until they are fluffy and smooth. Add the eggs one at a time, beating after each addition. Beat in the yogurt. Add the dry ingredients and blend them in thoroughly. Pour the batter into the prepared pan. Bake for about 40 minutes or until a cake tester inserted into the center comes out clean. Let the cake cool in the pan for 10 minutes then invert onto a cake rack to cool completely. Serve plain or with ice cream, sorbet, or Yogurt Sauce. Makes 8 servings.

Yogurt Sauce

½ cup whole milk yogurt, plain or vanilla

½ cup heavy whipping cream

1 tablespoon sugar

Place the ingredients in the bowl of an electric mixer. Beat at medium-high speed until the mixture stands in soft peaks.

Place the bowls and beaters in the refrigerator for 15 minutes before you make the sauce. It will make the sauce thicker, quicker.

Strawberries with Balsamic Vinegar and Mascarpone

Balsamic vinegar's sweet and tangy taste makes it useful for desserts as well as salads and entrées. This dessert is perfect on a summer's eve when you can buy good seasonal berries. I know that many people look for the largest strawberries they can find, but I actually prefer the smaller ones because they are usually sweeter. I also buy strawberries only when they have a floral fragrance that I can detect before I even pick up the container or stand near the bin. If you are ever lucky enough to buy wild strawberries, don't miss the opportunity; these little claret-colored gems are sweeter, juicier, and more intensely flavorful than any cultivated variety.

> 1 quart fresh strawberries, cut in half
> 3 tablespoons brown sugar
> 3 tablespoons plus 1 teaspoon balsamic vinegar
> ½ cup mascarpone cheese
> ½ cup whipping cream
> 2 teaspoons sugar
> Mint leaves

Wash and drain the strawberries and place them in a bowl. Add the brown sugar and 3 tablespoons balsamic vinegar. Toss and let macerate for 1 hour (or as much as 4 hours). Place the macerated strawberries in 4–6 serving dishes. Combine the mascarpone cheese, whipping cream, sugar, and remaining balsamic vinegar in a bowl and whip until soft peaks form. Spoon the cheese mixture in equal portions over the berries. Garnish with mint leaves. Makes 4–6 servings.

Spiced Oranges

Orange flower water is a flavoring popular in Middle Eastern cooking. It has a delicate but definite citrus taste. This dessert is lovely as is, but you can also serve it with sorbet or ice cream. I particularly like this after a spicy meal.

3 large or 4 small navel oranges
1 teaspoon orange flower water or ½ teaspoon vanilla or
    orange extract
2 teaspoons confectioners' sugar
¼ teaspoon ground cinnamon
1 tablespoon minced fresh mint
2 tablespoons finely chopped toasted almonds
Mint leaves for garnish

Peel the oranges and cut them into thick slices. Remove the white pith from the outer edge and slice the fruit into rounds. Place on a serving platter. Drizzle with orange flower water. Using a sifter or small strainer, dust with confectioners' sugar. Sprinkle with cinnamon and mint. Scatter the almonds on top of the fruit. Garnish with fresh mint leaves. Let rest for 15 minutes. Makes 4 servings.

Orange flower water is distilled, like brandy, but is alcohol-free.
Vanilla (and other) extracts usually contain alcohol, although there are brands that don't.

Clove and Lemongrass-Poached Plums

Here's a way for you to use the fibrous, outer leaves of the lemongrass stalks that you would normally discard (I also add lemongrass leaves to the pan when I roast chicken). Save the tender, inner core for recipes like the Thai-Style Fish Curry (page 99). Lemongrass leaves suffuse the poaching liquid with a gentle, lemony quality, more complex but not quite as strong as lemon peel.

½ cup sugar
16 whole cloves
Outer leaves from 1 large stalk lemongrass (4–5 leaves)
2 pounds Italian prune plums

Place the sugar, 1½ cups water, cloves, and lemongrass leaves in a saucepan large enough to hold the plums. Bring the liquid to a boil over high heat. Lower the heat and simmer for 10 minutes. Add the plums. Cook for about 10 minutes or until the plum skins split and the fruit is soft. Remove the pan from the heat and let the plums cool in the syrup. Serve the plums with some of the poaching liquid. Makes 4–6 servings.

There's a lot you can do with this simple dessert.

- Serve the plums with lemon sorbet and garnish with fresh mint leaves.
- Strain the poaching liquid and boil it down to a syrupy consistency, let it cool and serve the plums with the reduced poaching liquid.
- Serve the plums with sweetened mascarpone cheese: 1 cup cheese mixed with 2 tablespoons sugar and 1 tablespoon minced fresh ginger.

Italian prune plums are dark-purple skinned, with green insides. They are first-rate for poaching because the flesh is firm and holds up well when poached. They are also sweet, unlike most varieties that tend to be tart. And they're a good size as well. One small prune plum fits snugly on a dessert spoon and equals one mouthful. The season is short though— late summer. Take advantage while you can! Substitute 4 large black plums if you can't find the others (cut them in half and remove the pit).

The Grand Finale

My grandson Zev once put on pajama bottoms that had polar bears on them; the top had stars and stripes. When asked why he combined the two he said he wanted to wear the "grand finale, you know when all the fireworks happen at the end of the show." These cookies are like that. Inspired by a recipe of Laura Bush, they combine oatmeal raisin cookies and chocolate chip cookies and there's also a bit of coconut just for fun. A truly grand finale to any meal. I always keep a batch in the freezer and when I run out of them, everyone complains until I bake another batch.

1 cup all-purpose flour
1½ teaspoon baking soda
1½ teaspoons baking powder
1½ teaspoons ground cinnamon
½ teaspoon salt
¾ cup unsalted butter or margarine, softened
¾ cup packed brown sugar
¾ cup sugar
1 large egg
¼ cup orange juice
1½ teaspoons vanilla extract
1½ cups quick-cooking oats
1¼ cups chocolate chips
1 cup dried flaked coconut
1 cup chopped almonds
¾ cup raisins

Preheat the oven to 350°F. Mix the flour, baking soda, baking powder, cinnamon, and salt in a bowl. Combine the butter, brown sugar, and sugar in a large bowl and beat them with an electric mixer set at medium speed for about 2 minutes or until creamy and well blended. Add the egg, orange juice, and vanilla extract and beat them in thoroughly. Stir in the flour mixture until just combined. Stir in the oats, chocolate chips, coconut, almonds, and raisins. Scoop blobs of dough about 2 inches in diameter and place on lightly greased cookie sheets. Bake for 15–18 minutes or until browned. Makes 3 dozen cookies.

You can freeze these in plastic bags and eat them cold and hard, without defrosting.

MISCELLANEOUS BASICS

This chapter includes a few recipes that are served with or included in other dishes, but are generally useful for your other recipes too. Garlic Toasts (page 225), Pita Crisps (page 225), and Croutons (page 224) are all-purpose crispy breads that can serve as snacks or as garnishes or textural elements for soups or salads. Harissa (page 228) is a condiment and Ras el Hanout (page 227) is a spice blend; both are wonderful, fragrant seasonings for many dishes. Lemon Tahini Sauce (page 226) is a favorite in Middle Eastern cooking, a versatile spread for sandwiches or sauce for cooked meats and vegetables.

Croutons

Croutons are a gastronomic whimsy. But these little cubes of bread can make a huge difference to a dish by providing texture contrast and flavor. They're usually strewn into salads, but they are also wonderful on top of soup and casseroles. You can make stuffing out of them, tuck them into an omelet, dip them into hummus or just nibble them as a snack. Packaged croutons are often hard as rocks and loaded with salt and additives. If you have extra time, try making your own. It takes just a few minutes.

> 2 slices firm home-style white bread
> 2 tablespoons butter, margarine, extra virgin olive oil,
>   or a mixture

Trim the crusts from the bread and cut into small cubes. Heat the butter in a sauté pan over medium heat. When the butter has melted and looks foamy, add the croutons and fry them, tossing frequently for 4–5 minutes or until they are lightly browned and crispy. Makes about 1 cup.

Croutons can be baked instead of fried: Preheat the oven to 400°F. Brush both sides of the trimmed bread with the butter and cut into small cubes. Place the bread cubes on a cookie sheet and bake for about 8–10 minutes or until lightly browned and crispy. Stir occasionally during baking.

If you like herbed croutons, sprinkle the buttered bread with ½ teaspoon mixed dried herbs before you cook them. For cheese croutons, add 1½ tablespoons freshly grated Parmesan cheese.

Garlic Toasts

These are so easy, useful, and versatile you'll be adding them to lots of different dishes, where they'll give a finished quality to whatever you're cooking. Garlic toasts add crunch to salads—see how special plain lettuce and tomato is when you tuck a toast or two on the plate. Or lay the toasts on top of hot soup. Or use them as an hors d'oeuvre base for such diverse items as tomato salad, hummus, tzadziki, or even canned sardines or anchovies.

> 8 slices Italian or French bread cut 1 inch thick
> 1 garlic clove, cut in half
> 3 tablespoons extra virgin olive oil
> 1 tablespoon minced fresh herbs (or 1 teaspoon mixed
>   dried herbs), optional

Rub both sides of the bread with the cut garlic clove and brush both sides with the olive oil. Scatter with optional herbs. Toast the bread lightly. Makes 8 slices.

Pita Crisps

Pita crisps make a wonderful snack and they're also perfect on top of salads or soups and as an accompaniment for dips.

> 1 (8-inch) pita bread
> 1 tablespoon extra virgin olive oil
> Sea salt or kosher salt

Preheat the oven to 450°F. Brush both sides of the bread with the olive oil and sprinkle with salt. Cut each pita into 8 wedges and place the wedges on a cookie sheet. Bake for about 3 minutes per side or until crispy. Makes 8 pieces.

Lemon Tahini Sauce

This is a good all-purpose sauce for meats, poultry, fish, and vegetables. I also use it as a spread for sandwiches.

½ cup sesame tahini
⅓ cup lemon juice
3 tablespoons minced fresh parsley, preferably flat-leaf
2 medium garlic cloves
½ teaspoon salt, or to taste

Place the tahini, lemon juice, parsley, garlic, and salt in a blender or food processor and blend until smooth and creamy. With the motor still running, gradually add 4–6 tablespoons water, using enough to make a thick, smooth sauce. Makes ½ cup.

Quick Ras el Hanout

Ras el Hanout is a Moroccan spice blend that is so fragrant, flavorful, and useful I always have a supply in my pantry (I keep it in small, airtight containers). The words mean "top of the shelf" and translate vaguely as "the best spices" you can buy. It's an aromatic, robust mixture but it's subtle too. Just a bit adds color and complexity to plain dishes such as rice, couscous, or sautéed vegetables. It's also terrific as a spice rub for grilled lamb and poultry.

1½ teaspoons ground ginger
1 teaspoon salt
1 teaspoon freshly grated nutmeg
1 teaspoon ground cumin
1 teaspoon ground turmeric
1 teaspoon ground cardamom
¾ teaspoon ground allspice
¾ teaspoon ground cinnamon
½ teaspoon freshly ground black pepper
½ teaspoon ground mace
¼ teaspoon saffron threads
¼ teaspoon ground cloves
⅛ teaspoon cayenne pepper

Mix ingredients thoroughly. Makes about 3½ tablespoons.

Always keep dried herbs, spices, and spice mixtures in a cool, dark place away from the heat (inside a cabinet that's not near the oven).

Harissa

Harissa is a Tunisian condiment used throughout North Africa and the Middle East. Just a bit of it gives a delicious energy to sauces, soups, stews, marinades, and dressings. Spoon a bit over couscous or fried eggs. Use it on a sandwich. This spicy mixture will make dozens of foods taste even tastier.

¼ cup dried red chile peppers
3 medium garlic cloves
1¾ teaspoons caraway seeds (or 1¼ teaspoons
   ground caraway)
1 teaspoon ground coriander
¼ cup extra virgin olive oil

Place the chile peppers in a bowl, cover them with boiling water and let soak for about 30 minutes. Drain the peppers but reserve the soaking water. Place the peppers in a small food processor with the garlic, caraway seeds, and coriander. Process, scraping the sides of the bowl occasionally. Add the olive oil and continue to process for a minute or two, scraping the sides of the bowl occasionally. Add 2–3 tablespoons of the soaking water and process to make the sauce as smooth as possible. Store the harissa in a covered container in the refrigerator for up to 3 months. Makes about ¼ cup.

Schug is similar to harissa. It's a specialty of Yemen and contains hot peppers, garlic, and spices. You can buy both harissa and schug in jars; they are widely available.

You can use harissa to perk up vinaigrette dressing or mayonnaise. Add as much as you like, starting with a teaspoon, and blend it in thoroughly. Harissa vinaigrette is terrific on bean, chicken, or fish salads or on plain roasted peppers. Harissa mayonnaise makes a delicious spread for chicken or grilled vegetable sandwiches, or on fish burgers. It also jazzes up egg or potato salad quite nicely.

ACKNOWLEDGMENTS

Writing this book has been a delightful and delicious experience. But I could not have done it without the help of many others to whom I am indebted. First thank-yous go to my agent Michael Bourret at Dystel & Goderich Literary Management, who believed in this project, and to Matthew Lore at Perseus Books Group, who understood my vision and accepted the idea.

I am also grateful to my family: my husband, Ed, my daughters Meredith and Gillian and sons-in-law Gregory and Jesse, my brother, Jeffrey, and sister-in-law, Eileen, and my cousins Leslie and Neil who tested, tasted, helped clean up, and encouraged me every step of the way. Thanks to my grandchildren, Zev, Lila, and Nina, just because.

I am heartily grateful to Rabbi Joshua Hammerman, the spiritual leader of Temple Beth El in Stamford, Connecticut, for guiding me through the complexities of kashruth, for answering all my questions and for underscoring the spiritual connection to food and eating. Rabbi Hammerman also introduced me to two other key people to whom I am indebted: Dr. Behjat Syed, who helped me navigate and understand Muslim halal, and

Donna M. Rosenthal, executive chairman of CLAL, the National Jewish Center for Learning and Leadership, for her enthusiasm and many, many good suggestions.

To my friends Jean-Louis Gerin, owner-chef of Restaurant Jean-Louis in Greenwich, Connecticut, and Rebecca Martin and Judy Roll, chefs at the Stamford JCC, thanks for the recipes you shared with me.

Thank you also, Collin Tracy, project editor, and Lara Comstock, copy editor, and everyone else on the hardworking Perseus Books Group team who helped make this book a reality.

To Rob Pace, thanks for tasting, for honest feedback, and for helping to keep me in shape even during the writing of the chapter on desserts. And thank you to all the workmen, repairmen, postal workers, and others who had occasion to be in the house when I was cooking and who sampled, nibbled, and offered opinions about the food.

INDEX